ARCHITECTURE IN PROCESS

ARCHITECTURE IN PROCESS

Edited by James Steele

A.R. ACADEMY EDITIONS

Cover: Thom Mayne's Blades Residence project, Santa Barbara, California: preliminary sketches; *Page 2:* Steven Holl's Museum of Contemporary Art project, Helsinki, Finland: interior view from museum entrance of the ramp leading into the sequence of intertwining spaces

Photographic Credits
Matsuo Photo Atelier: pp54, 55; Tom Bonner: pp90 (*below*), 91 (*below*); Todd Conversano: pp132, 134-135, 136-137, 138-139, 140-141; Magdalena Glen: p99; Paul Groh: pp112, 113, 114-115, 117, 119, 121; Peter Mackinven: p25; Mark McVay: p86; Tomio Ohashi: pp72-73, 74-75, 76, 77; Kinga Racon: p111; Guiziano Zampi: pp20, 21
All illustrative material is courtesy of the architects unless otherwise stated.

House Editor: Maggie Toy
Art Editor: Andrea Bettella
Designer: Jan Richter
Editor: Natasha Robertson

First published in Great Britain in 1994 by
ACADEMY EDITIONS
An imprint of the Academy Group Ltd

ACADEMY GROUP LTD
Editorial Offices
42 Leinster Gardens London W2 3AN
ERNST & SOHN
Hohenzollerndamm 170, 10713 Berlin
Members of the VCH Publishing Group

ISBN 1 85490 306 3 (PB)

Distributed to the trade in the United States of America by
ST MARTIN'S PRESS
175 Fifth Avenue, New York, NY 10010

Printed in Italy

Contents

James Steele
Drawing to Displacement

Books about architecture typically focus on form rather than process; the final result is given precedence over the laborious search to achieve it. Regardless of the fact that the post-industrial age is now well underway in most of the 'developed' world, and the transformation of previously well-established institutions that has taken place as a consequence is now taken for granted, built artefacts continue to be presented as the primary items of interest in publications about them, with graphics, in a completely finished state, relegated to a position of secondary importance, if they are included at all. The existence of such selection, as Noam Chomsky has suggested, is due to the 'intelligentsia', who mediate between those who conceive each artefact and the general public, creating what he has called the 'ideological justification for social practice', as well as the aesthetic standards implicit in such selection.[1]

Current indications of an increasing awareness of the need for communal rather than individual initiative at a global scale seem not to have affected this interchange, either due to habit or presumption. The last vestiges of the condition of modernism still encourage patterns established over a hundred and fifty years, and environmental prerequisites inexorably continue against this sombre dichotomy, or rather in spite of it. There is presently an inordinate fascination with the way great architects create. This interest is especially among students and young practitioners who hope to decipher, in the first diacritical markings of origination, the unequivocal confirmation that the elusive mystical force variously called 'inspiration', or 'conceptual insight' which they suspect have been present at the inception of all significant works of art, is alive and well and still equally valid.

Judging from the work presented here, which is part of the selective mentality that Chomsky describes, rationalised by the comparisons between different approaches that such a choice affords, the instinct to continue what Eric Owen Moss has described in his parody of Le Corbusier, as an 'outpatient search' is still strong.

A Preference for Pictographs
In his monumental work on Egyptology, Polish archaeologist RA Schwaller de Lubicz has observed in *The Temple in Man*, how the two ancient riverine cultures of the fertile crescent developed pictographic writing at about the same time, through painstaking mimetic accumulation. He differs from other authorities, however, in his substantiated belief that, while the increasing pressures of agrarian organisation encouraged a transfer to cuneiform notation in Mesopotamia, the Egyptians concurrently opted to retain their hieroglyphic system, out of respect for tradition, and a preference for symbolic, rather than linear expression.[2]

There is a direct parallel to this preference in the way that artistic

canons in each culture evolved, with Egypt retaining and perfecting strictly regimented techniques that prohibited foreshortening and obscured physical characteristics in favour of a descriptive, two dimensional analysis, in which each aspect was shown in its entirety. Out of this variance emerged two diametrically different world views, with architecture that reflected each. While there are apparent parallels in religious and mathematical constructs, there are important distinctions in the way that each were related to their respective societies, with those of Egypt's being more anthropocentric, and those of Mesopotamia being decidedly abstract. The 'Babylonian Map of the Sky' Eric Owen Moss so frequently refers to, is a sophisticated analogue of the Egyptian myth of Nut, the elongated goddess whose body was felt to intermittently protect the sun disc in the repetitive course of its diurnal passage. In its insistence on the importance of convention, Pharaonic Egypt was asserting its belief in national and cosmic cycles, prompted by a vivid reminder of these in the more predictable surges of the Nile, which was not restricted by a deeply cut channel. The comparison achieved by De Lubicz for an appreciation of the close connection that exists between language, graphic expression, world view and architectural style, was confirmed in copious Semitic studies following Ferdinand de Sassure.

A Dialectic of Representation
As in the Pharaonoic period, there remains little or no indication that Gothic builders, who alas relied on strict canons, and rule of thumb geometry, used any drawings, in spite of a popular image typified by an illuminated rendering in a Bible Moralisée of the time, showing God as divine architect, circumscribing the earth with a huge compass. The secrets of the Bauhütte, obscured from a populace that was eager to help construct the cathedrals that the masons devised, were of the same kind as those used by the Pyramid builders who achieved remarkably accurate and sophisticated engineering feats, with extremely crude instruments and no drawings, that we know of. The guilds, as the refuge of the tradesmen who assisted in cathedral construction, and the conservatory of handicrafts, were weakened, as Peter Bürger has explained, 'around the beginning of the sixteenth century because of the new seigneuries and principalities on the one hand, and wealthy cities on the other, [which] became sources of an ever-increasing demand for qualified artists who were capable of taking on and executing important orders'. The result, Bürger states was that: 'this increase resulted in a loosening of the guild ties of the artists (the guilds were an instrument of the producers by which they protected themselves against surplus production and the fall in price this entailed).'[3]

The range and extent of these 'important orders' on commissions, and the impact that they had on artists, who typically in the Renaissance worked in all fields of endeavour, cannot be emphasised too strongly. Indeed by the time Bramante and then Raphael began work on the reconstruction of St Peters, office organisation, of the type used by architects today, as well as the successive sets of drawings they employ, had then been established. The cartoon, which now has a far less serious connotation, was as necessary as a first step in this succession as it was the organisation of a painting, indicative of a process by which, in the course of the next three centuries, art, including architecture, music, theatre and literature, began to be seen as autonomous, rather than as a part of a social context, as they were in medieval life, produced in a creative vacuum separated from the pragmatics of daily life.

The perception of the autonomy of the artist in that relatively brief period became firmly entrenched. The 'invention' of perspective, as a corollary to this process, is also an important indication of such separation, since, as Robert Hughes, Peter Eisenman and many others have observed, it is an artificial construct, based on abstraction, which promotes a detached, idealistic view-point, as opposed to reality. Rather than presenting the world as we actually see it, which is more akin to the fragmented sets of images in a David Hockney collage, perspective is formulated around a motionless 'station point', the individual as observer, aloof from all surroundings.

Point, Line and Plane: the Relevance of Dimensionality

It is not coincidental that the advent of writing is taken as the beginning of civilisation and the connection between graphic preference and cultural identity so evident in Egyptian hieroglyphics and art is present, in varying degrees and in numerous contexts, both during and since that time. The end of the present century is a poignant reminder of another such example, in the West, in *fin de siècle* Vienna, where aesthetic sensibilities have been traced to historical forces, subliminally predicted in personal ways, that were soon to rip the Austro-Hungarian Empire apart.

Gustav Klimt and Egon Schiele, as two of the most distinct mediums of those premonitions, were as diametrically opposed, as Egypt and Mesopotamia, and may be seen following Adolf Loos' criteria, as the modern, individualistic equivalent of these ancient cultural groups. They are popularly viewed as stylistic opposites, and yet have much in common. Klimt is best known for his voluptuous, decadent figurative rendering in which pregnancy is literally used, as it was in the late medieval and Renaissance Europe, as an anagram of feminine completion and the termination of a world order which has finally run its course. Schiele, on the other hand, depicts tortuously thin, pubescent waifs in a majority of his drawings, or otherwise studies himself. In stark contrast to the fullness of the figures painted by Klimt, in which the third dimension is either implied or overstated, Schiele reveals, for the first time since Rembrandt or Dürer, the significance of line, as a description linking up the points of demarcation that separate humanity, in whatever condition, from nature, in either its benign or threatening state.

While undeniably different, both commentators have managed to capture the spirit of an age, in both its fullness and finality, through curvature and line, while still showing the same cultural heritage and an obsession with the most basic instincts of life. They show that drawing, especially in the form of the cartoons that became the basis of Renaissance architecture and art, is nothing more than seismographic shorthand; the outer manifestation of inner vision, however particular it may be.[4]

The Dilemma of Production

The working drawings of the contemporary architectural office, which are part of the contract with the client, are the final step in a series of 'production' drawings, now increasingly done on computers. The conversion of architecture as art to business, which was begun in Bramante's office, is now complete and as a business the profession must produce. The education of the profession, also needed to run this industry, is now a big business of its own, in spite of its relatively brief life span, with the Ecole des Beaux Arts as a primary model. The Ecole, which has passed on innumerable, often unrecognised traditions to the profession, also established many in regard to presentation drawings, which were so laboriously constructed as to qualify as architecture in their own right. I have vivid memories, as a student, of my first ascent up the stairs of the University of Pennsylvania Library, designed by Frank Furness, to the room where Louis Kahn held his Masters' class, and of the large gouaches that hung on the walls, dating back to the time when Paul Get taught there. Those drawings were part of the Beaux Arts system, just as Kahn himself was, but it has taken a lifetime for me to realise the full implications of that connection. Kahn's sketches, which may in many ways be seen as the beginning of the current wave of interest in drawing for its own sake as an isolated phenomenon in architecture, become increasingly reflexive and yet were always part of the commodity syndrome to which those presented here also belong. Kahn was a High Modernist, the last of the 'masters', and this was a period, as Frederic Jamieson has pointed out, that existed in parallel with a culture fed by mass commodity.

Other opinions about this connection aside, Modernism shunned commercialism, because of a similar distancing from the utilitarian, pragmatic world that took place in the Renaissance atelier, and yet was also a part of it, as the artists who sold their work to Florentine patrons were. Modernism sought to rise above commercialism, but was inherently bound to it. As Eagleton has said: 'Modernist works are in contradiction with their own material status, self-divided phenomena which deny in their discursive forms their own shabby economic reality.'[5]

Architects Without Architecture

With the exception of those represented here, there has never been a time when so many reputations have been made on so little work. Competitions are won on the strength of drawing alone. Yet when the time comes for completion, designs are found to be unbuildable as originally presented – if the prospect proceeds past competition stage. For some with the most inflated reputations, gained primarily through drawings, the realisation of even modest commissions, of a restaurant, bar or fire station, is cause for a media feeding frenzy, accompanied by unprecedented amounts of hype. This disproportionate fanfare is indicative of several factors, aside from the most obvious distortion it represents. There has never been such a wide dichotomy between graphics and construction; where architecture has historically been accomplished with a minimum of drawing, that medium has now supplanted, or at least become equal to the artefacts it represents in a wide segment of the public consciousness.

The fashion, for architects to be artists begun with Le Corbusier and Kahn, was most notably perpetuated by Michael Graves, who not only began by exaggerating the five points, but their author's graphic style as well. Richard Meier uses collage as a mental stimulus to three dimensional visualisation, and Aldo Rossi, whose spare 'De Chirico style' is as evocative as his stripped down, unornamented architecture, which sells equally well.

The current generation of those who use this mixture has expanded dramatically, for reasons that go beyond economic necessity. It would be simple to ascribe this trend to the recession that began in the late 1980s, now shown to be a general economic readjustment throughout the 'developed' world, which is symptomatic of the shift from an industrially based economy to an information, or service based economy. The reasons go deeper, to the shift itself, and the revolution this has caused in the way that people in a post-industrial society see the world. Baudrillard, in his examination of the 'hyper-real', has touched on that shift, which is related to the persuasiveness of the media, and television in particular, in the less than fifty years that its influence has been in effect. Instead of art imitating life, as it once did, life now imitates art, or television, movies, magazines and advertising in general.

Marshall McLuhan's predictive prophecy, that the media is the message, has not only come true but has now been superseded by a phenomenon of superficiality beyond his original thesis. To re-word the significant re-adjustment proposed by Baudrillard, it would be more accurate to say that art imitates life which imitates art, in a continuous spiral in which reality has become progressively elusive, if not impossible to determine at all. By emphasising graphics, certain architects, as mediums of the media, are simply conduits of that shift. In an ironic and curious way, they approximate an eastern view, that by possessing a picture of something one actually possesses the thing itself.

Virtual Artificiality

All of this has been further complicated by the computer, which has been part of a revolution of its own. The advances made, and the possibility of using it as an aid for design, have been spectacular, to the extent that many professional schools require students to buy them. Indeed, there is little hope of employment without such skills. For the Los Angeles contingent represented here, who flatly reject the idea that Frank Gehry has been a stylistic influence, there can be no doubt that he has set an example in his willingness to move into the electronic age in high gear and he has accomplished this transformation in short order. He is a particularly good example of the complications presented to the artist/architect by the potential of the electronic dimension, because he, above all others in his generation, has consistently made a point of the importance of effecting a marriage between the two disciplines, and has strenuously tried to do so himself. His self-identification with the Constructivist aesthetic, as well as with the group that became associated with the Ferus Gallery in the 1960s is well known, as is his willingness to collaborate with artists, such as Claes Oldenburg and Coosje van Bruggen in the design of the Chiat Day Headquarters on Main Street, Los Angeles. What has yet to be fully analysed, however, is the extent to which he has embraced computer technology, which has both been adapted to his style, and has dramatically changed it.

Typically working from spontaneous sketches, which are then passed on to others who interpret them into three-dimensional models, Gehry has tended to abjure drawings in the traditional sense, relying on his visceral, sculptural and intuitive ability to develop the initial model. This is transferred into the documentation required for tender and construction when the more tactile process of cutting and pasting is complete. The problems presented by that transfer had represented a nightmare for the young apprentice in the office, who had used triangulation, projection, pantographs and grids in ways unchanged from the techniques used by sculptors during the Renaissance, until a decision to build a full scale portion of the Disney Concert Hall wall, for the 1992 Venice Biennale changed all that. The insurmountable difficulty of producing the shop drawings necessary for the stone cutters and the miscellaneous metal workers to produce the section in the short time available, forced the office to consider other innovative alternatives, leading to digitalisation of the kind used in the aero-space and automotive industries, where a hand-held probe transfers complex modelled curves to the computer screen. This not only allowed the section of wall to be produced on time, but also convinced the client and the contractors of the Hall that it could actually be built within a reasonable budget, especially since the computer could actually be programmed to cut the stones.

The result of this liberating breakthrough for the Gehry office has been revelatory with a noticeable shift having now occurred. Monumental, seamless curves, rather than the broken surfaces that were once in favour, are now the order of the day. Project teams, surrounding large cardboard models with digital probes in hand, connected to space-age control rooms in the distance, are lined up along the cavernous recesses of the office, producing buildings that all look disturbingly homogeneous.

Thom Mayne, who has tended to rely on graphics as a means of conceptual evolution, taking satisfaction in the expressive capacity of drawings to reveal possibilities, as well as to explain complex mental constructs, spoke recently of his need to convert to computer technology, also because of a pressing deadline. His entry, in a competition for a national museum in Tours was accomplished entirely in this way, and he is determined to expand in this direction. However, this concern that the final presentation looked too mechanical and slick, untouched by the human hand, is a refrain constantly heard today – the contemporary equivalent of the concerns expressed by Ruskin and Morris about the machine. Because the machine, especially following the demise of the Bauhaus, eventually prevailed, there have been no architectural Luddites this time, and yet the nagging concerns, about the future of the profession, and the role that drawing will have in it, continue to grow, especially among those who have relied so heavily on the medium. As Robert Delevoy has said: 'It may well be that the growing interest in what lies beyond the visible, in discontinuity of meaning, in the rearticulation of mimesis, has its origin in the desire to defend sensibility, feeling and the body against unbridled nationalism, the debunking effect of electronics, the statistical relationships and apocalyptic prospects of the post-industrial age.'[6]

Architecture on Trial

These concerns, about the seeming inevitability of the predominance of technology in a profession that has had a long history as a manual, apprentice-taught trade, imply an equal concern about the continuing purpose of drawing as well and are symptomatic of a wider 'crisis of conscience'. The separation discussed earlier, that pulled architects away from their traditional social context and encouraged them to become reliant on individual patronage, has resulted in a progressive state of isolation, and abdication of cultural responsibility. The sequencing of such disenfranchisement is extensive, with various aspects, such as architects' self exclusion from the popular housing market as described by Denise Scott Brown, having been well documented. The forced retreat, into the isolated, imaginary world that the pen or pencil makes possible, may in some ways be seen as a means of escape from this harsh reality; but it is also, in those places where contractors and structural engineers have now appropriated the services once provided by the architect, the sole remaining means of affirming what this profession does best, which is to think in three dimensions.

As Eric Owen Moss' brilliant studies show, some are more inclined to do this than others. More than anyone else today, he deserves, and has appropriated, the time honoured title of 'geometer', once applied to builders such as Anthemeis of Tralles, who designed the Hagia Sophia. In fascinating contrast to fellow 'Angeleno' Thom Mayne, who begins with similar sketches seen here extensively, for the first time, Moss continues to constantly evolve the spaces he sees in his mind. These begin at an unparalleled level of sophistication and proceed from there into a Piranesian realm that few others have travelled. To an extent not applicable to the graphics of Will Alsop, Itsuko Hasegawa and Steven Holl, who approach this dimension in a more plastic, painterly way, Moss relies heavily on drawing as an exploratory device, his own 'Babylonian Map of the Sky', and a careful study of his sketches read like successive entries into a personal diary written by someone determined to evolve.

This selection, then, is indicative of the variety of ways in which graphic media are used by architects, to explain, explore, reinterpret, translate and perpetuate their ideas, in the face of increasing technological supremacy. In a profession now seen by many as the final refuge of individuality, this media while it survives, serves as an unmistakable sign of that singularity, the signature of each person concerned. At a showing, recently organised by the Southern California Institute of Architecture (Sci-Arc) in Los Angeles, large numbers of drawings by architects were sold, to the surprise and delight of all concerned. Such a response may mean that the electronic revolution, which also threatens to make books such as this redundant, will only have a limited effect on an architect's need to draw, and the public's desire to observe. Along with publishers, who are betting that CD ROM will never totally replace the look and feel of a book, as a beautiful and informative object, there are those who feel that predictions about the demise of architectural graphics are decidedly premature. Whatever the outcome, the present need for a publication that provides an insight into what has hitherto been considered an impenetrable secret and mysterious process, has begun to be addressed here, in a provocative way, providing a behind-the-scenes look at the way architects think.

Notes

1 Noam Chomsky, 'Politics and the Intelligentsia', *Art in Modern Culture*, Francis Frascina (ed), Phaidon Press, London, 1992, p33

2 RA Schwaller de Lubicz, *The Temple in Man*, Devry Livres, Paris, 1983

3 Peter Bürger, 'On the Problem of the Autonomy of Art in Bourgeois Society', *Theory of the Avant Garde*, Michael Shaw (trans), Manchester University Press, 1984, p16

4 I am indebted to my son Christopher for this distinction.

5 Terry Eagleton, 'Capitalism, Modernism and Postmodernism', *New Left Review*, No 152, July-August, 1985, p45

6 Robert Delevoy, 'Polarity of the Symbol', *Symbolists and Symbolism*, Skira, Geneva, 1978

William Alsop
Cardiff Barrage, Cardiff, Wales

Design Process

Notwithstanding the efforts of all its staff to achieve the highest business standards, it remains William Alsop's belief that the significance of the practice is in its architectural convictions. Through its connections with specialist consultancies and with the industry, it has an awareness of the continuous upgrading and reinvention of building techniques and materials. The practice is eager to use new methods, but not for their own sake. When used appropriately, they can offer the possibility of achieving structural or environmental goals, of creating forms that were hitherto impossible to build. Alsop & Störmer believes that building methods, new or traditional, are only the means to define the nature of a place, and the experience created transcends the significance of any of its parts.

The practice's experience in the design of public buildings and spaces has confirmed its view that architecture, when positively designed, allows the most meaningful and communicative engagement with the public. William Alsop believes that every project begins with a return to first principles: 'The office has a completely open mind about what architecture is. This is not a closed question as far as we are concerned. There is a continuing exploration of form, colour, functional, social and behavioural issues. These investigations resolve themselves in

buildings and structure which offer a richer experience to both the user and the visitor. The client is considered an integral part of the design team. This is necessary in order to establish a base which will allow the project to step beyond the expectations of all who are involved in the design process.'

When asked about his specific process of designing a project he goes on to say: 'The work can only realise its full potential if I deliberately undermine my expectations and preconceptions. It allows me to see. My process of undermining employs different strategies including painting, talking and walking. The paintings in particular allow the work to evolve in a physical manner, which keeps it fluid and malleable. The paintings, or sometimes sketch models, then become a way of extending the concepts through conversations with both the client and the entire design team. The first part of the process is to design a conversation – not a building. Behind this is an idea about uncertainty. Uncertainty about the end product. I am using "uncertainty" or the unknown in a positive sense. It is our responsibility to explore what is not known before forming opinions or taking decisions. In order to avoid the trap of preconception, I prefer to talk about behaviour rather than functions. Behaviour is a less precise word which allows me to understand what people actually do in a building as well as what they are supposed to do. This allows the architect to consider the actual experience of a space. An experience that will lift the spirit.

By employing devices to open up our architectural vision, we do not forget previous experience. Although there is no fixed style, all work is an extension of previous work. All the work is one work. The thoughts, directions and explorations are used to find new relationships within new situations and placements – new projects. The client, engineers, quantity surveyors, et al, are treated as architects on the job. This allows the architecture to be discovered as opposed to designed. The process of discovery requires the design team to take the responsibility to enjoy change for as long as possible in the design and building process.'

All projects should be 'a matrix of possibilities' – this phrase encapsulates Alsop's philosophy.

The Cardiff Barrage project is a world first in the integration of major architectural and artistic involvement in large project engineering design. The Barrage is central to the overall plans to develop Cardiff Bay and its surrounding docklands. It is designed to create an enormous inland freshwater lake out of, what is now, tidal mud flats by creating a dramatic man-made barrier. The Barrage will complete the first phase of the connection of two historic buildings, the Pier Head Building and the Penrath Pier. The Barrage itself was designed to provide a visual extension of the local topography extending across the estuary. It has been carefully sculpted to provide an ever changing experience for the public that choose to walk one of the three interconnected pathways that run the mile plus length of the structure. The paths themselves change in dimension and undulate as part of the overall topography of the Barrage. These also provide rest areas and viewpoints along the paths. The combination of hard and soft landscaping elements with the strong architectural elements, such as the Lock and Sluice Control Building, the three Fishing Piers, each of a different design, and the brightly coloured Groynes, which are used to create enclosed, protected walled gardens, all combine to convert a serious engineering project into a major leisure facility for the area. Parts of the undulating landscape at the edge of the lagoon have been designed to become islands and peninsulas during periods of high water. Even the necessary functional elements, such as the fish pass, the sluice gates and licks have been designed to contribute to the interest and pleasure of the visitor.

The development of this project, from the competition entry to the final accepted proposal, demonstrates how the key concept was used as an axis around which the design was moulded in a continuous process until the final solution was reached. A solution which even now offers areas of potential change and development.

Architectural design by William Alsop, Alsop & Lyall Architects.

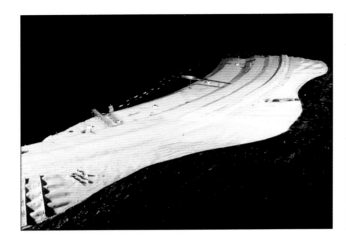
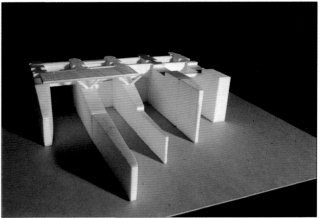

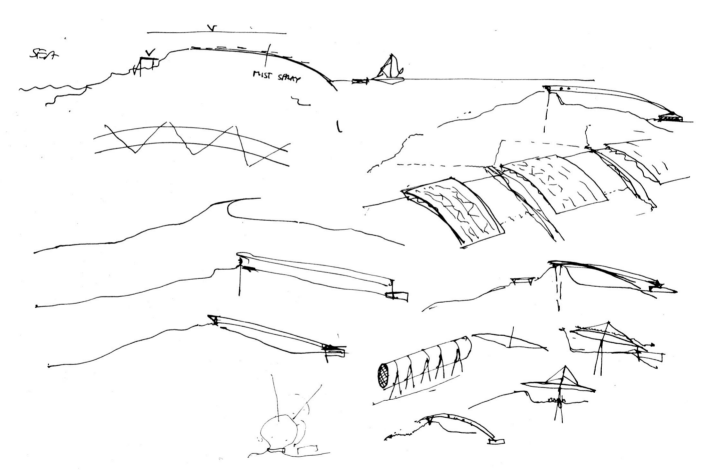

FROM ABOVE, L TO R: THE COASTLINE OF THE BAY, WHICH WILL BE SHELTERED BY THE BARRAGE, IS APPROX EIGHT MILES LONG; MODEL; THESE EARLY SKETCHES, BY ALSOP, ARE THE STARTING POINT FOR THE DEVELOPMENT OF THE SHAPE OF THE BUILDINGS, WHILE EXPLORING THE SPECIAL CONDITIONS OF THE SHORE

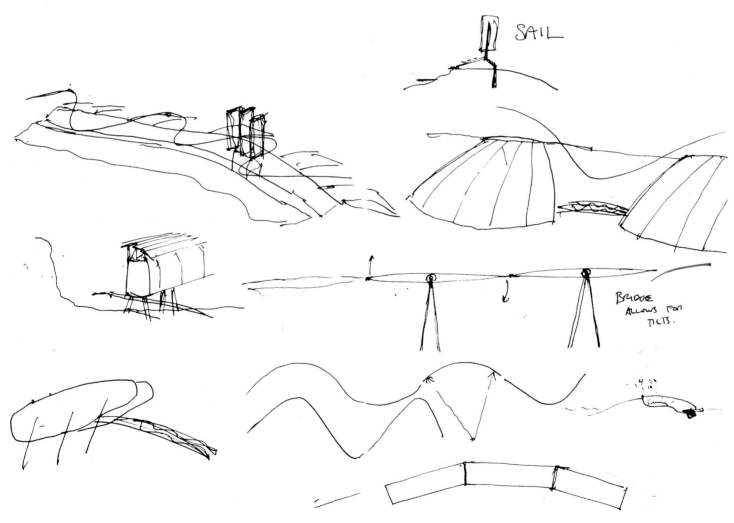

SAIL

BRIDGE ALLOWS FOR TILTS.

From Above, L to R: For the Barrage, an architecture that forms the surrounding for sophisticated technology was created; detailed studies of all eventualities of weather and water conditions were an integral part of the design process

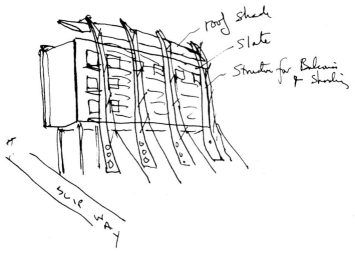

roof shade
slate
Structure for Balconies & Shading
SLIP WAY

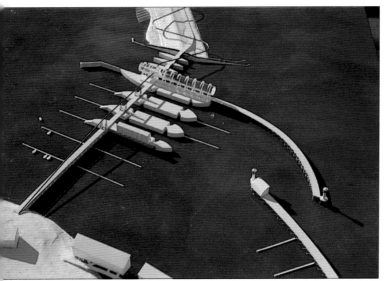

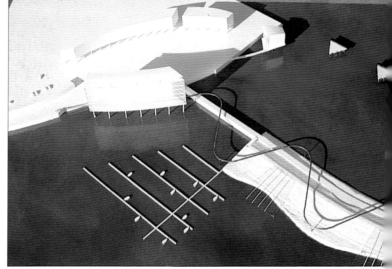

white steel coated.

CENTRE, L TO R: THE COMPETITION MODEL (SCALE 1:1000) SHOWS MANY FEATURES WHICH REMAINED PART OF THE FINAL DESIGN; SOME DETAILS, FOR EXAMPLE THE LENGTH AND SHAPE OF THE FISHING PIERS, WERE FURTHER DEVELOPED DURING THE DESIGN PROCESS AFTER THE COMPETITION WAS WON

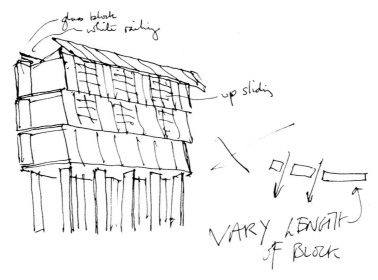

glass block
white railing

up sliding

VARY LENGTH
OF BLOCK

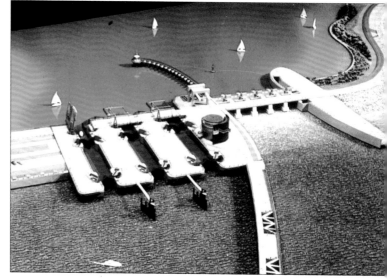

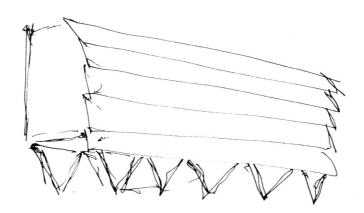

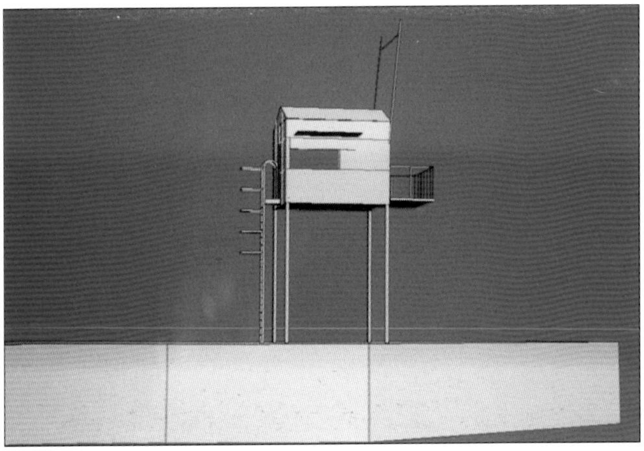

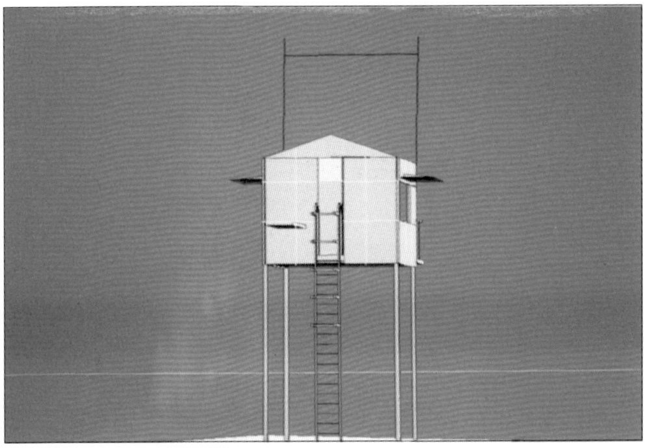

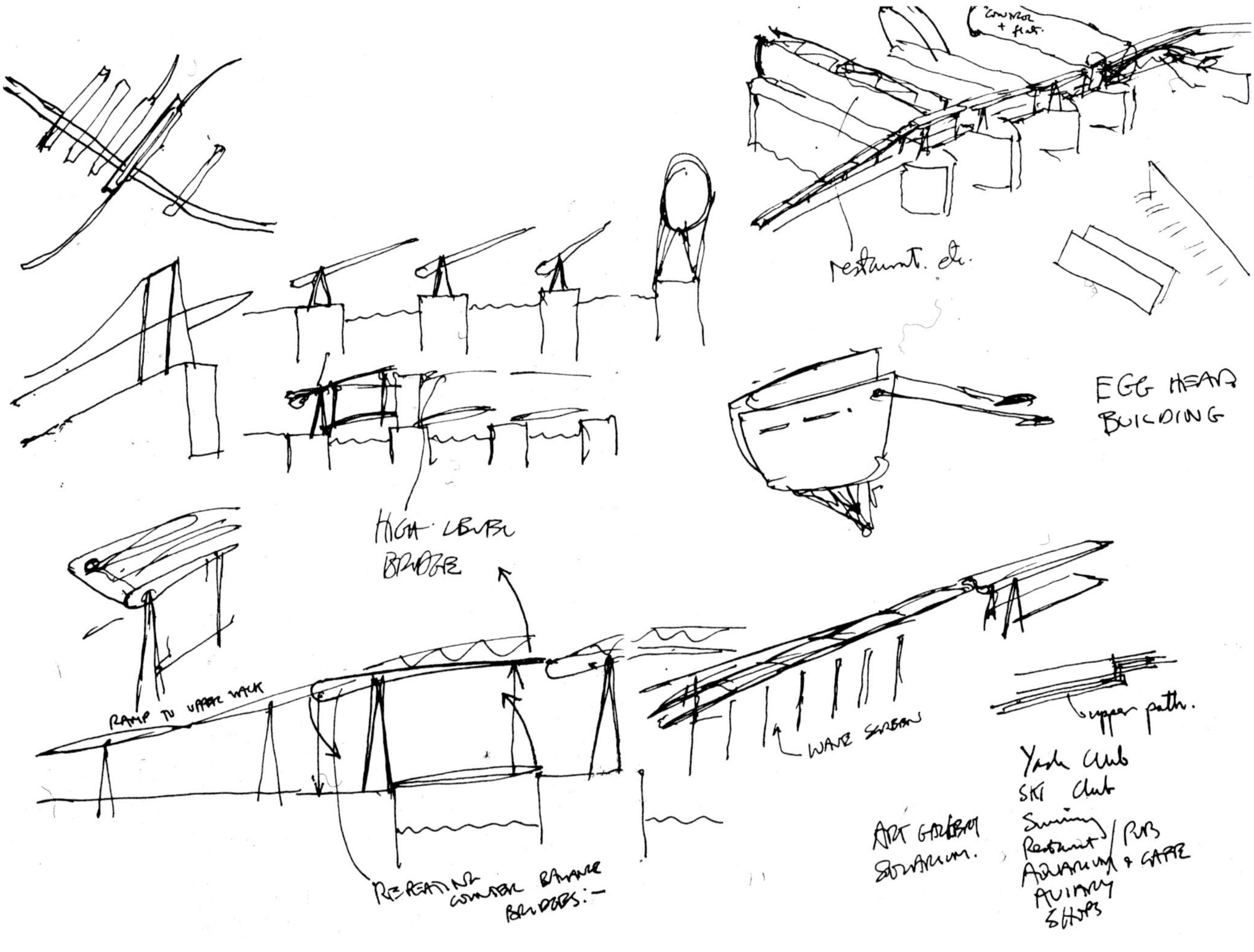
restaurant. etc.
EGG HEAD BUILDING
HIGH LEVEL BRIDGE
RAMP TO UPPER WALK
WAVE SCREEN
upper path.
REPEATING COUNTER BALANCE BRIDGES:-
ART GALLERY
SOLARIUM.
Yacht Club
SKI Club
Swimming
Restaurant / PUB & CAFE
AQUARIUM
AVIARY
SHOPS

From Above, L to R: The Yacht Start will be one of the attractions – yacht races will be held in the Bay on a regular basis; the building has facilities for flagging, as well as a small balcony for referees to view races; perspective studies exploring the scale of the yachts which will sail on the lake created by the Barrage

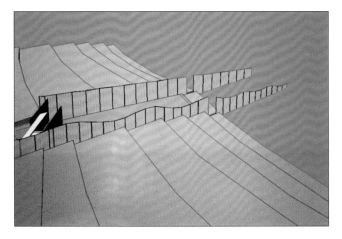
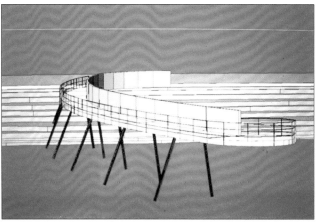

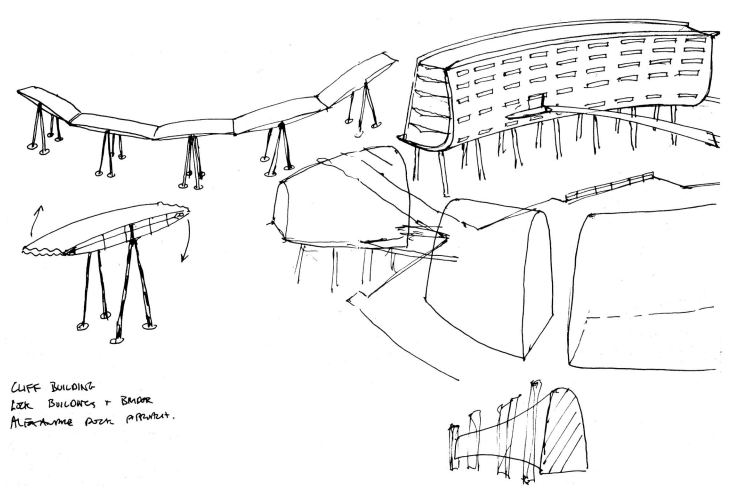

CLIFF BUILDING
LOCK BUILDINGS + BRIDGE
ALEXANDRE POZZI APPROACH.

From Above, L to R: The walled
garden will act as a shelter for rare
plants, which may otherwise not
flourish in the rough climate of the
shore; the fishing piers vary in length
and shape — at low tide, they allow
access for walkers and act as viewing
points for visitors; another example of
the care employed to carry out the
perspective studies

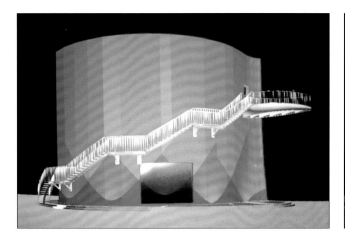
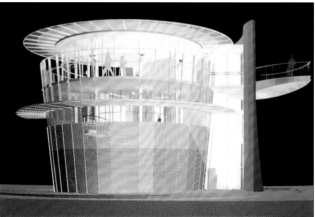

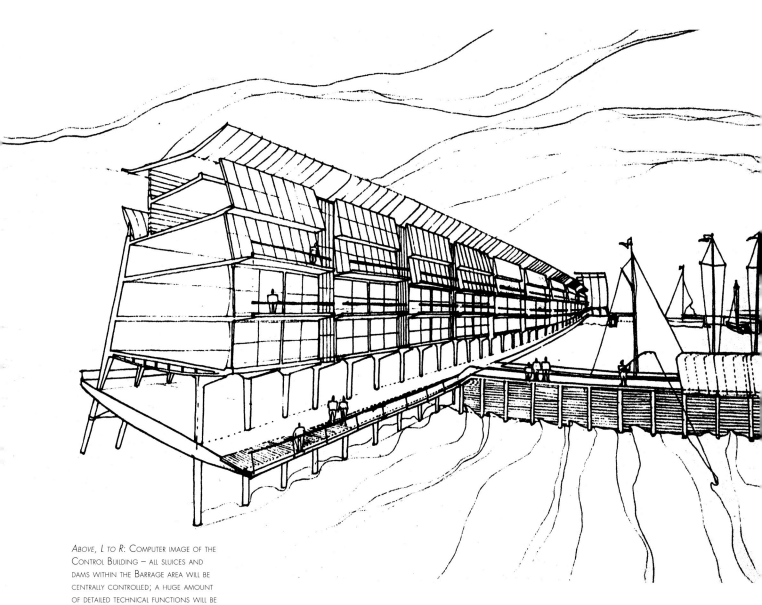

Above, L to R: Computer image of the
Control Building — all sluices and
dams within the Barrage area will be
centrally controlled; a huge amount
of detailed technical functions will be
necessary to maintain these central
control services

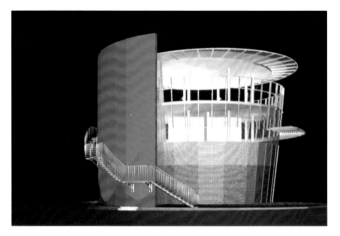

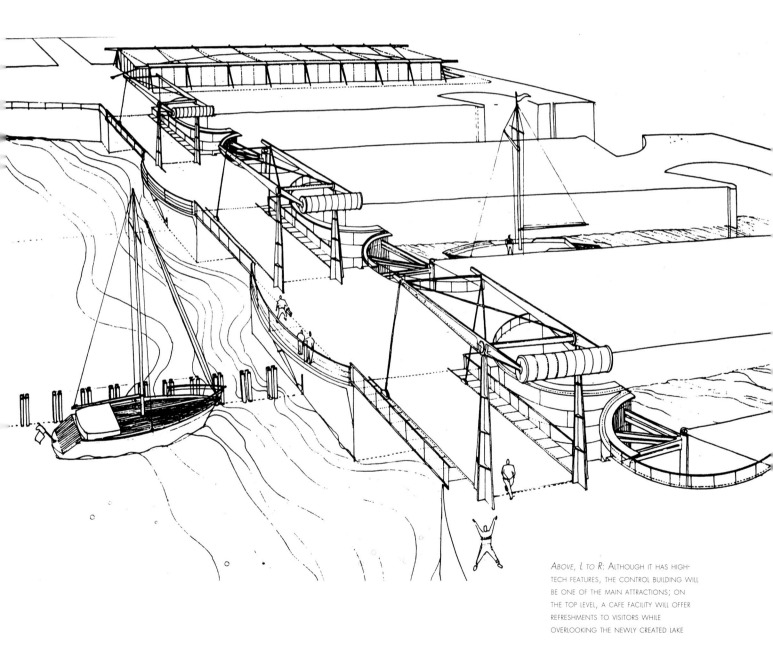

William Alsop
Hamburg Ferry and Cruise Ship Terminal, Hamburg-Altona, Germany

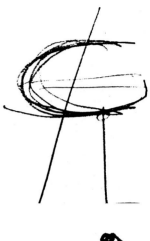

'This building gave us the opportunity to build by the water. What a piece of water! The Elbe flows with life and creates new images continuously. Sometimes it becomes aggressive and floods (approximately six times a year) to new proportions. Our building facilitates views of this mighty river from a safe haven. I know from having an office adjacent to the Thames, that continual views of water are not always welcome, particularly on melancholic February mornings. This can be overcome by concentrating on the quality of light in the building. There needs to be a subtle combination of lightness and cosiness. The building has eyelids on the south side. Sometimes it is necessary to close one's eyes to the external world. The building blinks as it creates an edge to help channel the Elbe. Every street needs an edge definition and in this respect the Elbe is not exceptional. Our street edge offers a line of parallel platform from which to both observe and hide from the River.'

In 1988 a two phased competition was organised for a building comprising a terminal for the ferry to England, a cruise ship terminal, offices and a restaurant in Hamburg-Altona. The contract was awarded with the first prize to William Alsop Architects, who gained planning approval in 1990. The project was phased in two parts: phase one consisted of the England Ferry Terminal, for Scandinavian Seaways; phase two covered the cruise terminal and office centre for GbR Kreuzfahrtcenter.

The Hamburg Ferry and Cruise Ship Terminal, located on the River Elbe, is and was meant to be a celebration of the edge of the River. When phase three is completed it will be five-hundred metres long, the longest office building in Europe, maximising and epitomising the city's long ongoing affair with the river and its connection to the sea. The creation of a building to reflect this relationship was the key consideration in the design and development of the project.

The waterside of the building is visually open to and embraces the river and shipping while the land-side is less so. The green glass walls overlooking the river reflect the colour and literally the patterns of the river, while the silver metal spandrel panels present a more solid face to the street. The exception is at the ground floor where double height glassing allows the visitor a clear view through the public areas to the water and ships beyond.

There is a car parking area under the cruise terminal (phase two) creating the effect of a moat spanned by bridges to give visitors access to that part of the building. The floors above are for administration and office functions. The cruise terminal is being used as office space for a limited period to allow for completion of the required mooring facilities.

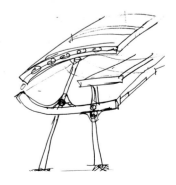

Other elements of the building have been designed or chosen to subtly remind the viewer of the importance of the river and sea to the city. The concrete 'A' shaped structural columns are reminiscent of the cranes and derricks along the quayside, but it is in the materials and details of the structure, such as the support for the viewing balcony, and other building elements, like the automatically adjustable sun visors, that the maritime feeling is really captured, while never becoming a pastiche. The structural system with the floors spanning between the exterior 'A' shaped columns allows for the provision of dramatic and completely flexible spaces. It is a site specific building in the best and total definition of that term.

The structure is made of a precast, reinforced concrete skeleton, with *in situ* concrete slabs. Elements included are: A-columns (inner column straight, outer side inclined), V-Beams (prestressed) and cantilevers (so called 'wishbones' supporting the north side roof to the ferry terminal hall, attached to the A-columns.

The roof structure and suspended gallery, in the six-storey part, is made from steel sections.

The building's facade consists of aluminium mullion and transom curtain walling elements with glass and white or silver aluminium panels. Computer controlled and manually adjustable solar louvres have been installed in the south facade.

Architectural design by William Alsop of Alsop & Lyall Architects.

FOR WILLIAM ALSOP, EXPLORATORY PAINTINGS ARE AN INTEGRAL PART OF THE DESIGN PROCESS, SOMETIMES THESE FILL JUST TWO SIDES OF A SKETCH BOOK, OTHERS ARE HUGE IN SCALE; *OPPOSITE*: THIS SERIES OF SKETCHES BY ALSOP SHOW THE DEVELOPMENT OF THE STRUCTURE FOR THE COMPETITION SCHEME. THE STARTING POINT IS A NEARLY ABSTRACT FORM, FROM WHICH THE ACTUAL SHAPE OF THE BUILDING DERIVES; *OVERLEAF*: EXPLORATIONS IN FORM FOR TWO PROJECTS AT EAST COUNTRY YARD, MADE AT THE SAME TIME AS THE FERRY TERMINAL DRAWINGS, SHOW THE INTERCONNECTIONS BETWEEN ALSOP'S WORKS, FROM WHICH UNIQUE BUILDINGS DERIVE. *PAGE 25, FROM ABOVE*: SKETCHES DO NOT ONLY CONTAIN WHAT ONE COULD CALL ALSOP'S ARCHITECTURAL PHILOSOPHY BUT ALSO DETAILS OF THE SCHEME, IN THIS EXAMPLE THE CHOICE OF MATERIALS; SECTION OF THE COMPETITION SCHEME; *OVERLEAF, FROM ABOVE RIGHT*: THE COMPETITION MODEL, WHICH IS SHOWN IN THESE IMAGES, WAS FOLLOWED BY THREE FURTHER DESIGN STAGES. THE BUILDING AS IT EXISTS TODAY WILL EVENTUALLY BE EXTENDED TO WHAT WILL BE EUROPE'S LONGEST OFFICE BUILDING

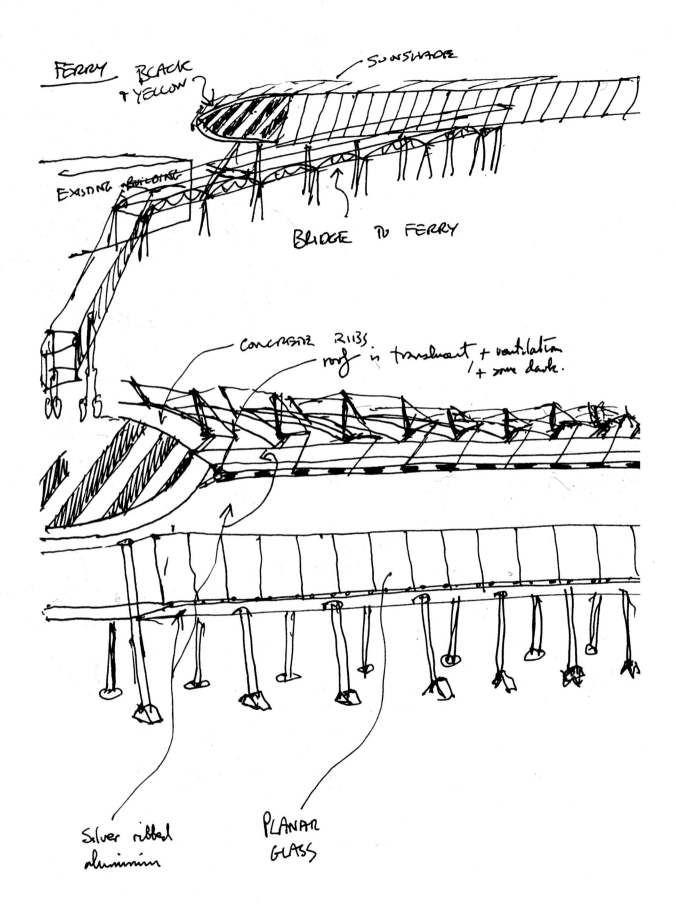

FERRY BLACK + YELLOW

SUNSHADE

EXISTING BUILDING

BRIDGE TO FERRY

CONCRETE RIBS.

roof is translucent + ventilation + some dark.

Silver ribbed aluminium

PLANAR GLASS

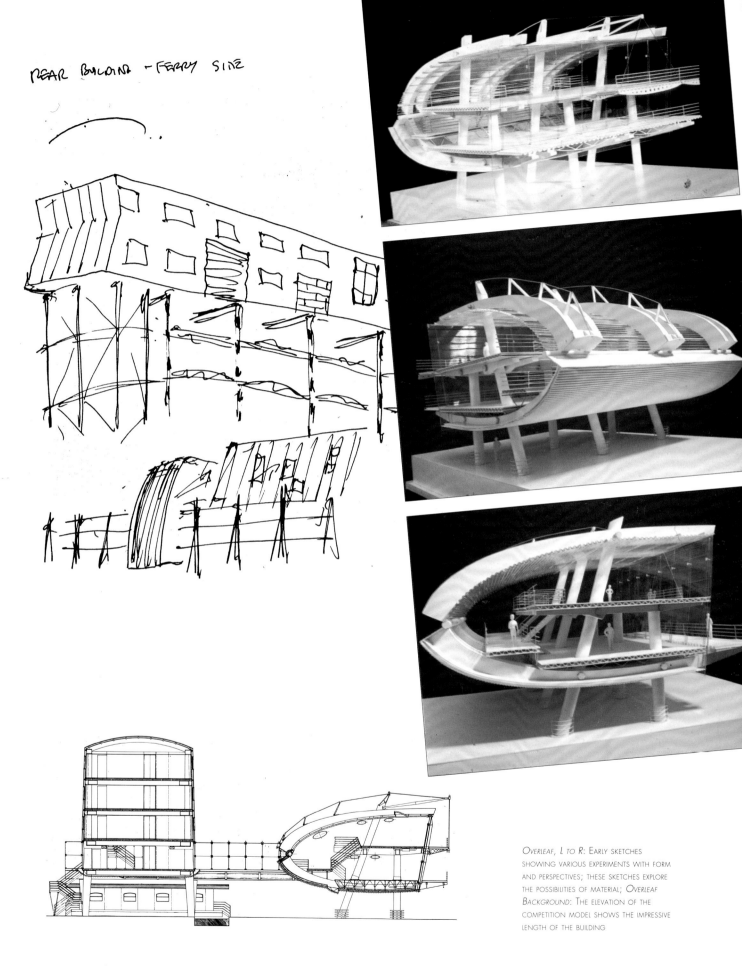

REAR BUILDING - FERRY SIDE

Overleaf, L to R: EARLY SKETCHES
SHOWING VARIOUS EXPERIMENTS WITH FORM
AND PERSPECTIVES; THESE SKETCHES EXPLORE
THE POSSIBILITIES OF MATERIAL; *Overleaf
Background:* THE ELEVATION OF THE
COMPETITION MODEL SHOWS THE IMPRESSIVE
LENGTH OF THE BUILDING

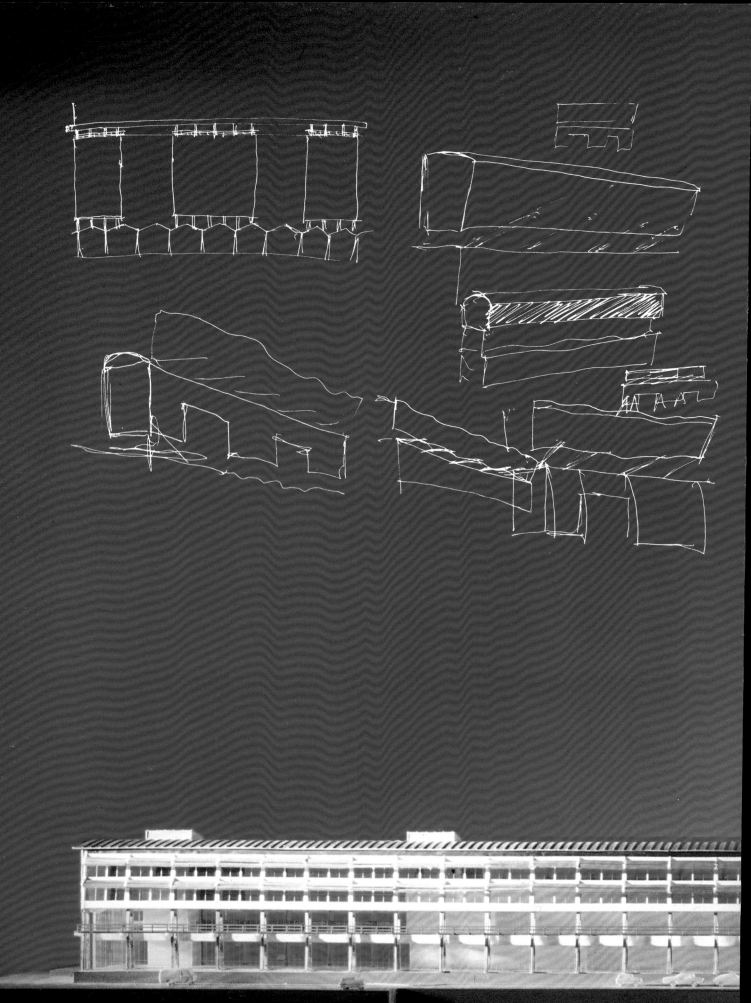

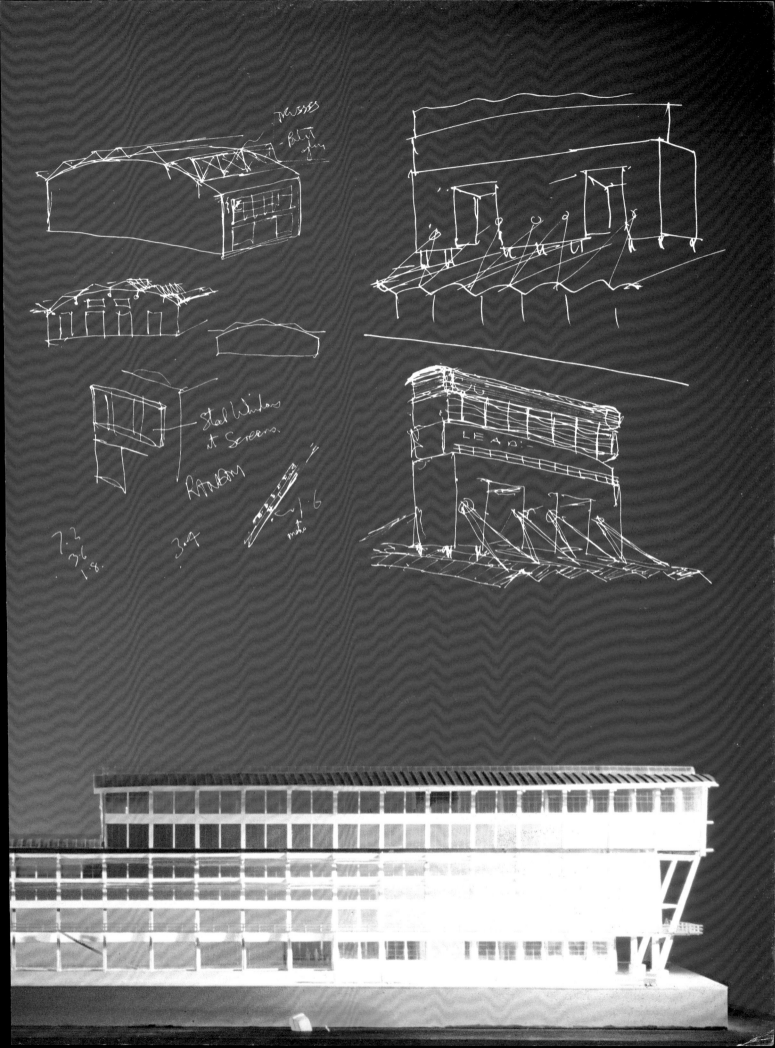

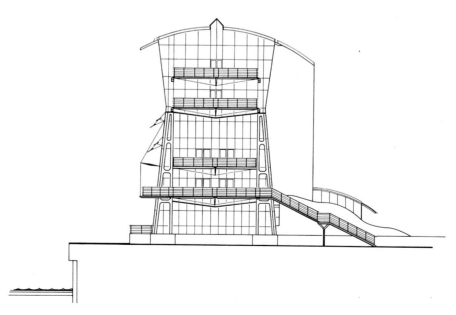

From Above: View towards the ferry
terminal from the former fish market in
Hamburg; elevation of east end facade
with steel balcony and public elevated
walkway

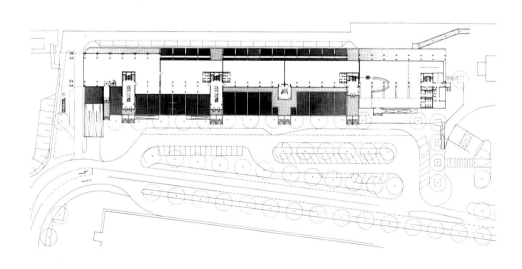

Itsuko Hasegawa
Shonandai Cultural Centre, Fujisawa City, Japan

The Shonandai Cultural Centre, 1991, is based on a proposal that won an open competition held by Fujisawa City. What attracted Itsuko Hasegawa to the project was the fact that it was a combination of a children's pavilion, community centre and public theatre. Public buildings have hitherto tended to be very formal, and she had been thinking even before the competition that such buildings ought to encourage people to drop by casually.

In explaining her entry to the competition jury, she wrote: '. . . in order to achieve its public objectives, the building must be a place that can bring together and adapt to many different classes of people: children and the elderly, women and men, the handicapped and those without handicaps. This should be thought of not as a single building but as a complex; one that provides a special place. This special place should have many different faces and be in constant flux. It should be able to accommodate multiple events and contain within it not only the world but the universe.' During this process, the difficulty of designing a public building sufficiently complex to accommodate a heterogeneity of views was impressed upon the architect. The entry, which expressed a strong concept, was made less assertive. It took on a group image and was transformed into a stage-set for the community.

On opening day, as on ground breaking day and all through construction, there was a gathering at which opinions were aired. Afterwards, a number of people told the architect about the roles they had played in the project. Among them were those who agreed with the view that the site should be covered with some two-hundred varieties of plants so that it would be like a giant ikebana reflecting the changing seasons, and that the planning of the surrounding community ought to incorporate this idea. This building therefore began to function as a landmark promoting environmental improvement.

The site is near Shonandai Station on the Odakyu Line, and is separated by the Fujisawa-Machida prefectural road from the Shonandai Park. The project is a cultural complex for the northern part of Fujisawa City. The area around the site, all developed through land readjustment, is becoming urbanised.

In thinking of the image that the building should project, Hasegawa considered what a public building in such an environment should be like. Firstly, part of the building, which in this context would have been conspicuous for its size, was buried. Hasegawa wanted to make the portion above ground a man-made park and enable all groups of people to use it, not just those with special reasons for coming to the Centre. The total volume of the facility is large for the site area. Two-thirds of it were fitted, and then buried, into a modernistic box-like structure to allow freedom of planning. In keeping with the theme of the Centre, which is to establish roots in the local community and to promote a better understanding of the world and the universe, spheres (a world globe, a cosmic globe, a moon globe and a geodesic dome) that suggest a futuristic, cosmic environment, and clusters of pitched roof structures, suggestive of woods or a village of folk houses, have been built above the ground. The plaza is a man-made garden with a stream, pond, greenery, various shelters and a path along which visitors can stroll through a roof garden. One can walk past a cluster of roofs, suggesting a mountain of rocks, the earth and cosmic globes. Devices that are activated by light, wind and sound, a tower of wind and light, and a 'tree' with a built-in clock, have been installed along the way. The rooms and corridor below ground face a sunken garden which admits light and fresh air and provides a clear path in case of an emergency One feels embraced by nature in this garden, where the wall has been plastered to suggest earth strata and where greenery has been planted.

For several years Hasegawa's practice has been based on the concept of architecture as a rebirth of nature, ie, another form of nature. Instead of thinking of architecture as something to be constructed according to reason and differentiated from other forms of matter, Hasegawa feels that architecture should be inscribed and legible in terms of the aspects of nature.

A basic theme of this project was to accept those things that had been rejected by the spirit of rationalism, the translucent world of emotions and the supple and comfortable space woven by nature, and to create a landscape filled with a new form of nature where devices enable one to hear the strange music of the universe.

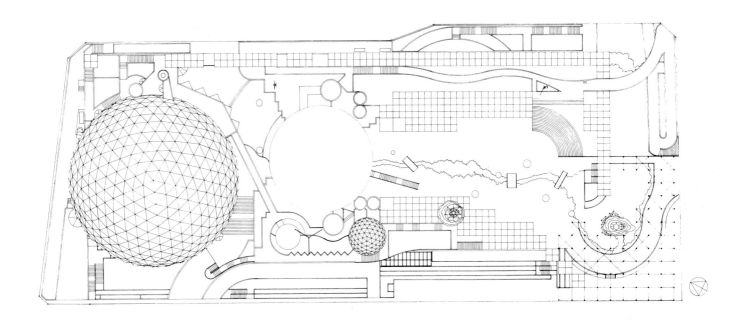

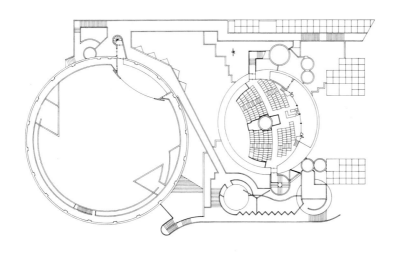

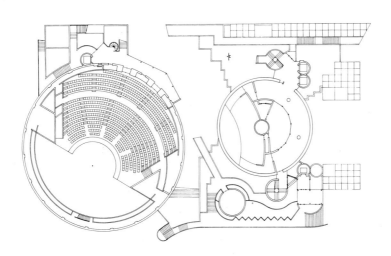

From Above: PLANNING THE HANGING
GARDEN WITH THE JAPANESE TOUR GARDEN
IN MIND; NAMING THE THEATRE
'(TERRESTRIAL) COSMOS', THE PLANETARIUM
'GLOBE' AND THE ATMOSPHERIC
OBSERVATORY 'MOON', 'INFINITUDE OF THE
UNIVERSE' AND 'THE SPACE WITHOUT THE
DEFINITION OF OUTSIDE AND INSIDE' –
THESE WERE THE MAIN THEMES OF DESIGN
AT THE THIS PHASE; HERE THE CHARACTERIS-
TICS OF THE THEATRE WERE BEING
CONSIDERED: A MULTIPOLAR, SPHERE-SHAPED
THEATRE, THE DOME OF CHAOS, THE
UNIVERSE WITH PEOPLE IN THE CORE;
Opposite, From Above: DESIGNING THE
GARDEN AND THE ARCHITECTURE AS A
WHOLE; DESIGNING THE PLAZA BY PLACING
THE POND, THE STREAM, AND THE
SUNSHADE ON THE GROUNDLINE;
PROPOSALS FOR THE EXHIBITS
OF THE CHILDREN MUSEUM, WHERE THE
HANDMADE GER (MONGOLIAN-STYLE
ROUND-SHAPED HOUSES MADE OF WOOD
AND CLOTH) ARE BUILT; *Previous Page*:
THIS SKETCH WAS DRAWN ON THE TRAIN
ON THE WAY BACK FROM THE FIRST VISIT TO
THE SITE, IN SEARCH OF THE IMAGE OF
ARCHITECTURE THAT IS ABLE TO MAINTAIN
THE VARIOUS ROLES OF THE OPEN FIELD THAT
THE SITE HAD FULFILLED IN THE LOCAL
COMMUNITY

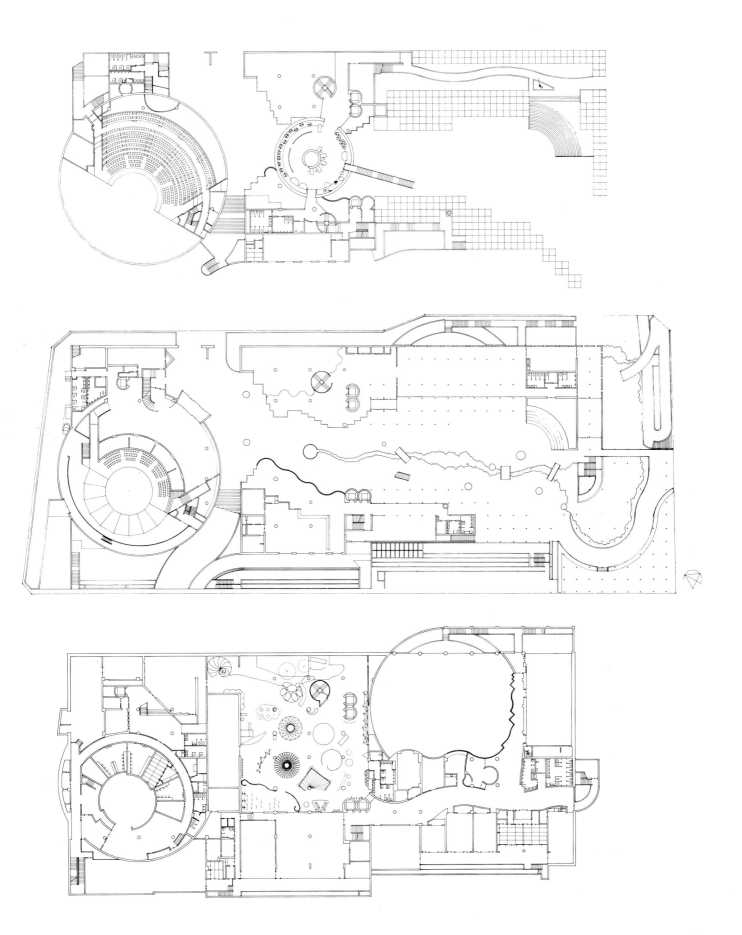

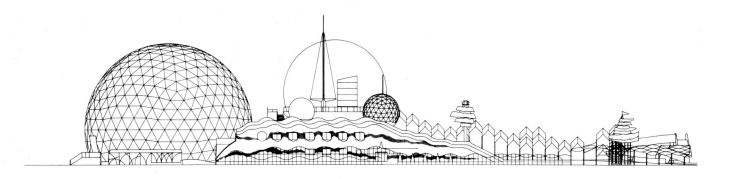

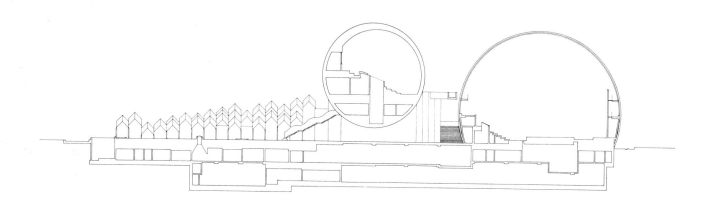

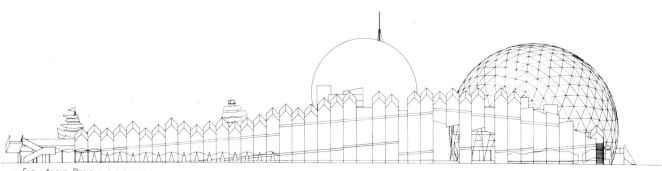

FROM ABOVE: DESIGNING THE WHOLE
SCHEME AS A SHIP WHICH CARRIES A SMALL
UNIVERSE; THE UNDERGROUND AREA HAS
BEEN REDUCED TO SEVENTY PER CENT OF
THE TOTAL FLOOR AREA AFTER MUCH
DISCUSSION WITH THE LOCAL USERS; THE
WALLS THAT MAKE UP THE HILL ARE THE
IMAGE OF THE COLUMNAR STRUCTURE OF
MERCURY STRATUM; *OPPOSITE*: FINALISING
THE DESIGN OF THE THEATRE. THE
ENTRANCE IS DESIGNED TO RECREATE THE
IMAGE OF 'FESTIVAL'

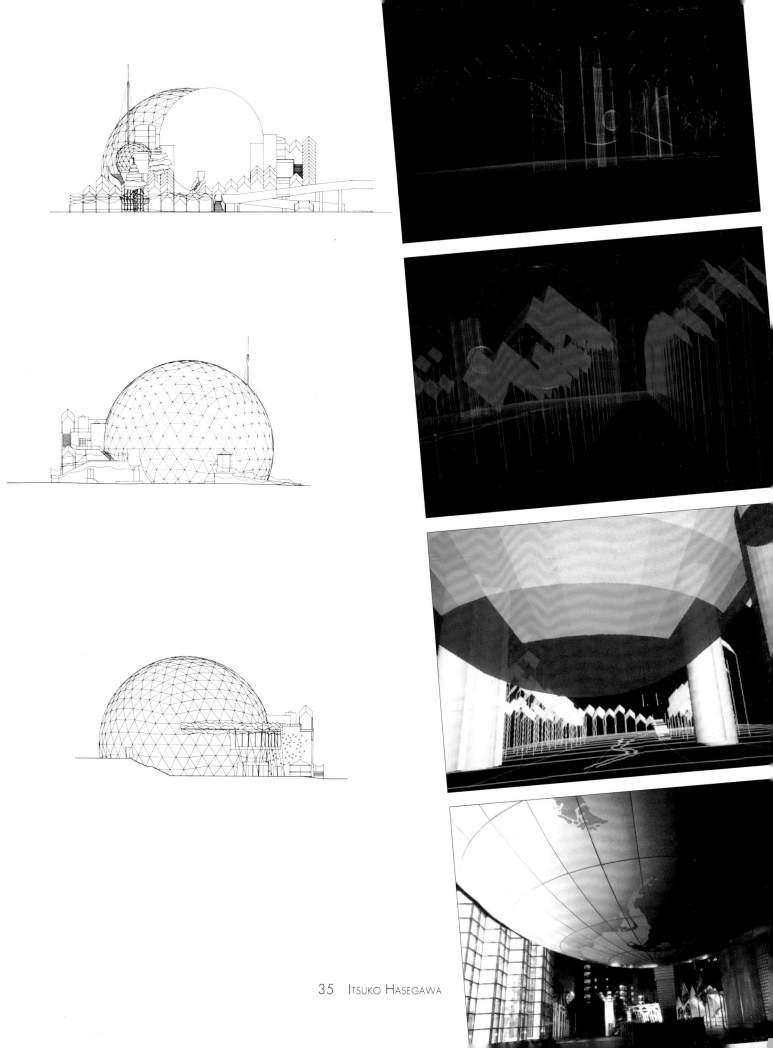

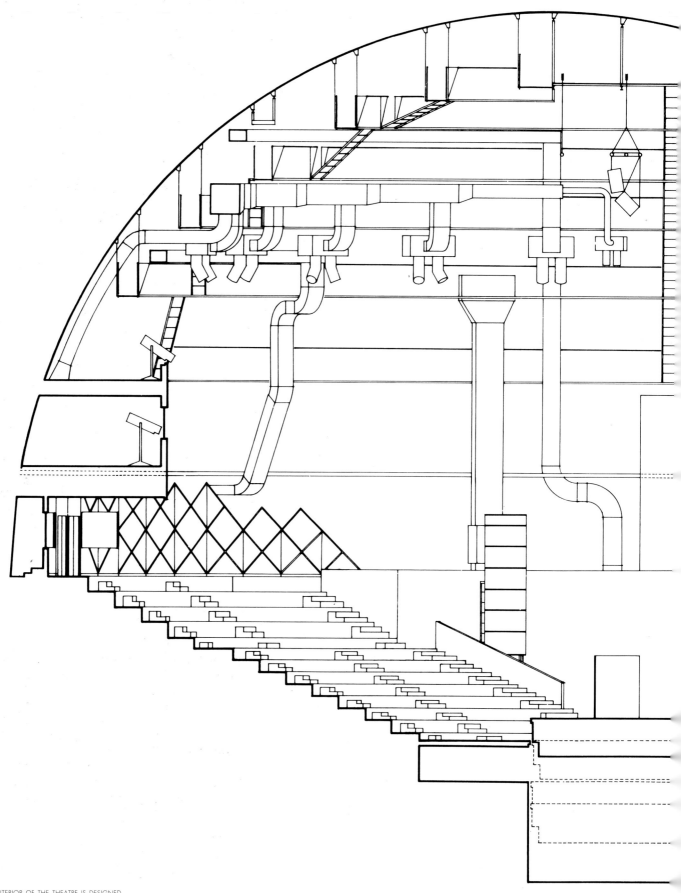

The interior of the theatre is designed as 'Latent Nature'

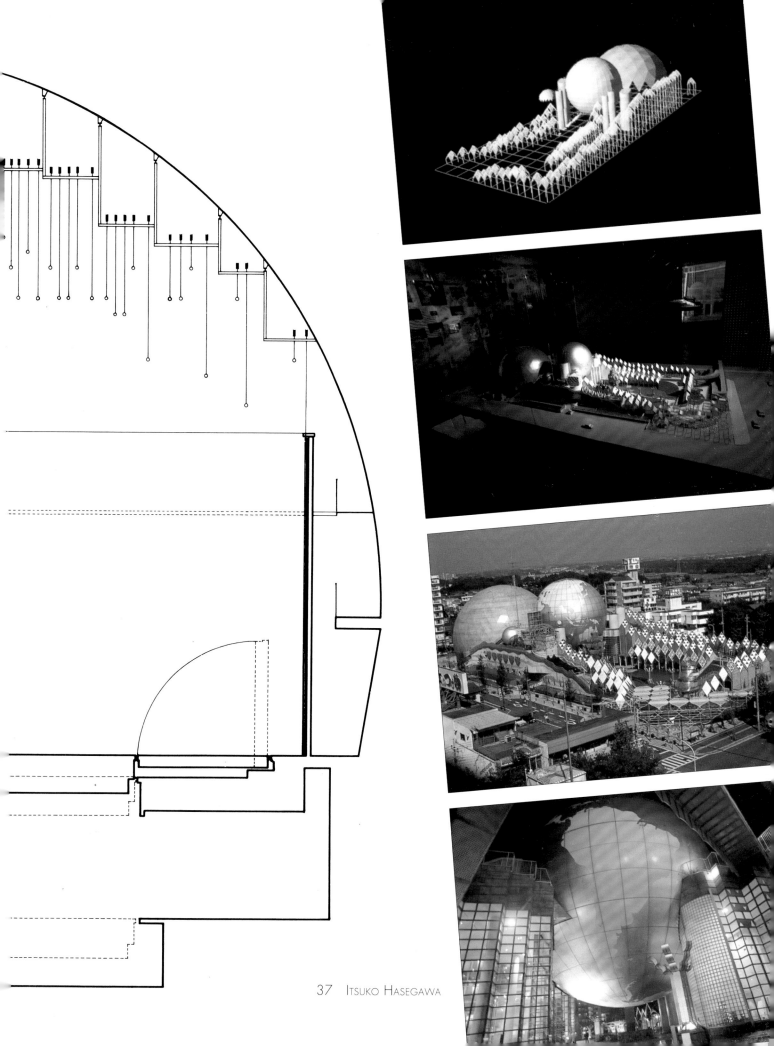

Steven Holl
Museum of Contemporary Art, Helsinki, Finland

The site for the new museum lies near the foot of the Parliament building, at a crucial intersection of the city grids. The overlapping geometry of the cityscape and the landscape is engaged in the architecture of the museum.

The primary curvature of the building is designed to engage the unique qualities of natural light in a latitude of sixty degrees north. The curved plan and section captures the warm light of a horizontal sun, controlling and diffusing it through carefully oriented apertures to distribute an optimum degree of natural light into the exhibition spaces. In relation to the increasing diversity of contemporary art, a wide variety of lighting conditions and exhibition spaces are provided throughout the museum. During the early evening hours of the winter months, glowing light escapes from the interior of the building, creating an inviting urban space.

The neutral and serene geometry of the gallery spaces provides the flexibility required for accommodating a broad range of contemporary exhibitions. The architectural language of the interior and exterior silences the intermediate scale such as columns, window openings and door mouldings. Between the large scale of the body of the building, and the scale of the detail, a neutral space is created for art. This architectural language allows the intermediate scale to be enhanced by the presence of artworks.

Entering from a new triangular plaza on the South, the visitor can immediately see all the main public areas and orientation points. All the galleries are connected by a circuit which can be used by walking up the ascending ramp in the lobby or by taking the elevator to the top of the building and walking down. The public stairs on each end of the building allow this route to be short circuited, which would be particularly useful during the installation of new exhibits.

Along the west face of the building, the cafe and the museum shop overlook a series of sculpture terraces. Natural stone walls define these 'roofless rooms' allowing diverse sculptural works to coexist in the outdoor landscape, visible to passers-by. A special intertwining urban passage adjacent to the reflecting pools provides a public walk from the northeast portion of the site to the southwest. This passage anticipates the completion of the master plan by creating an intertwining of nature, culture and the city.

STICH
SUTURE

CHASM
INTERCROSSING
INTERSECTING
A = OVERCROSSING

B. = UNDERCROSSING

RETICULE

X, CROSS, CROSSBONES CROSS

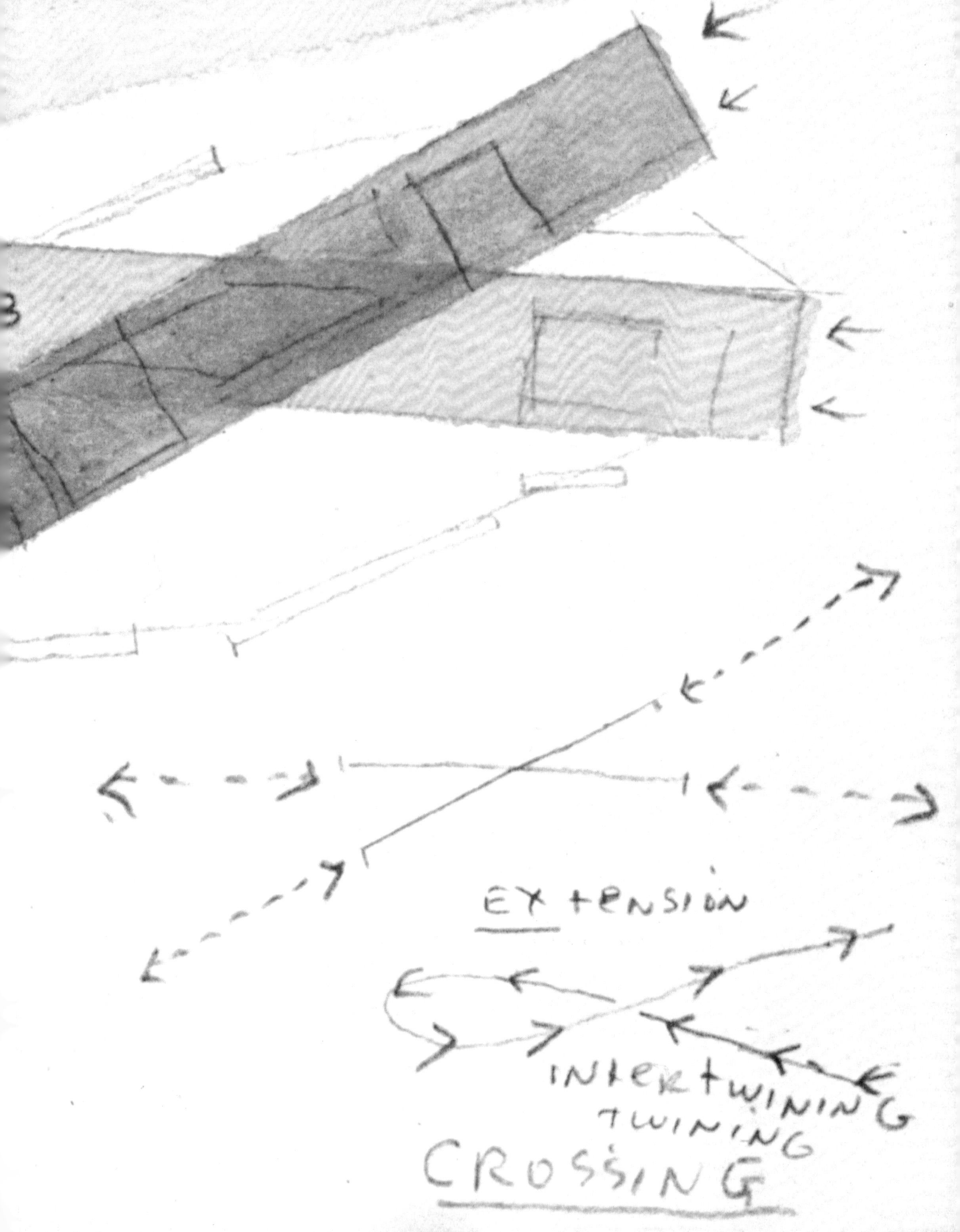

EXTENSION

INTERTWINING
TWINING
CROSSING

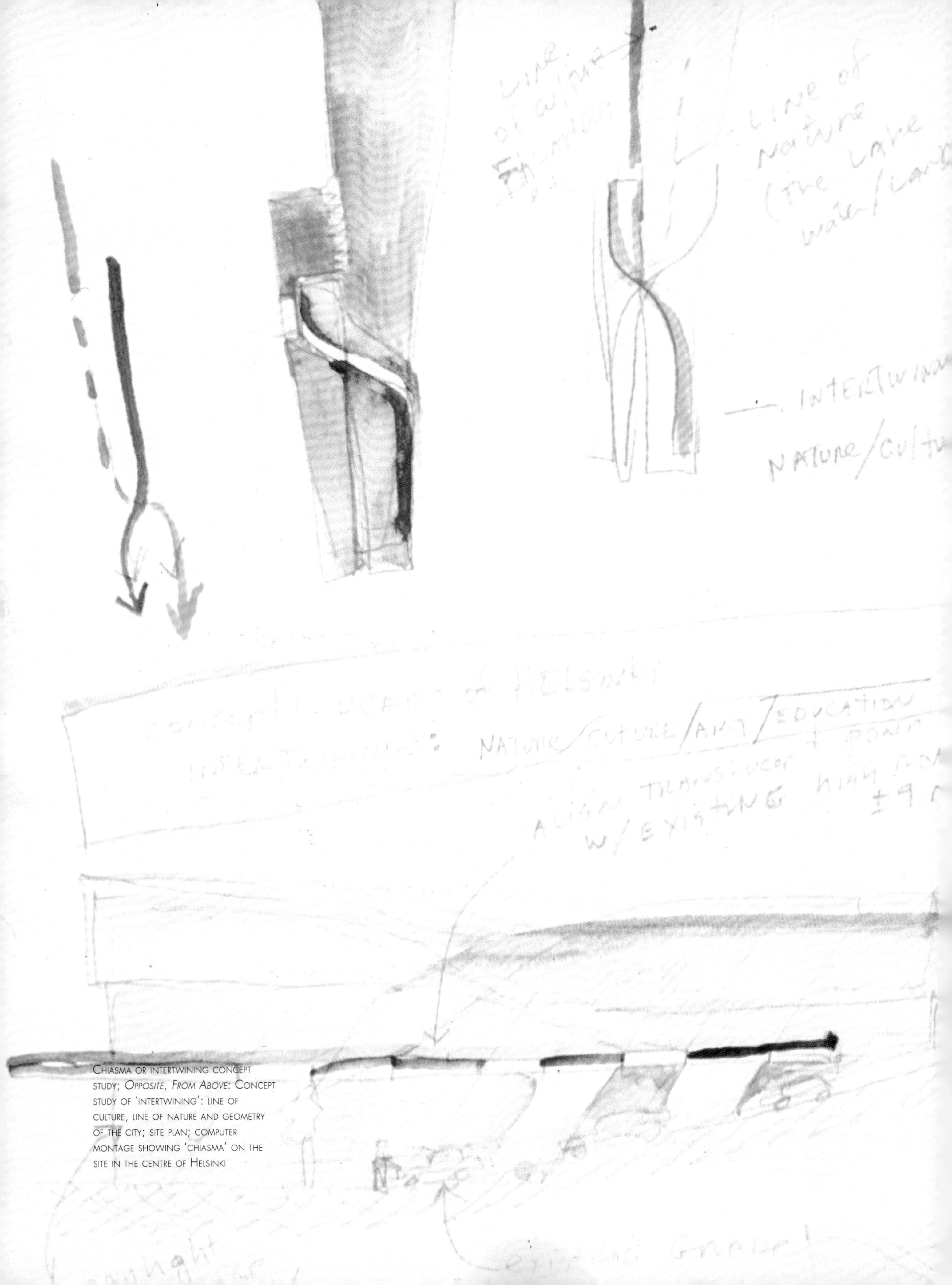

LINE of CULTURE FORMISM

LINE of NATURE (THE LAKE water/land

INTERTWINING NATURE/CULTURE

HEART of HELSINKI

NATURE/CULTURE/ART/EDUCATION

ALIGN TRANSLUCER + DOWN
w/EXISTING HIGH ±9

CHIASMA OR INTERTWINING CONCEPT STUDY; OPPOSITE, FROM ABOVE: CONCEPT STUDY OF 'INTERTWINING': LINE OF CULTURE, LINE OF NATURE AND GEOMETRY OF THE CITY; SITE PLAN; COMPUTER MONTAGE SHOWING 'CHIASMA' ON THE SITE IN THE CENTRE OF HELSINKI

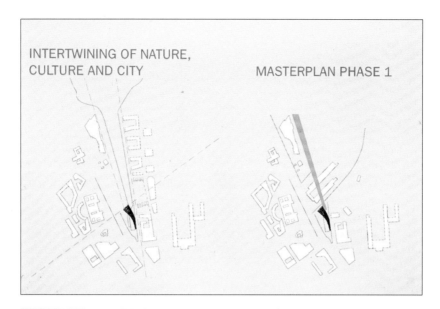

INTERTWINING OF NATURE,
CULTURE AND CITY   MASTERPLAN PHASE 1

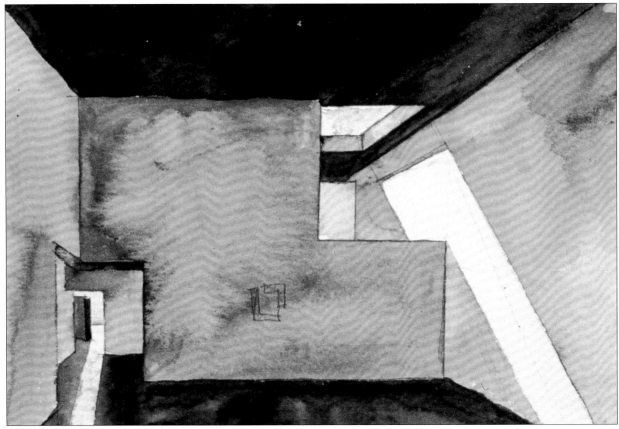

INTERIOR STUDY FOR THE GALLERIES: NEUTRAL SPACE FOR ART; *OPPOSITE*: INTERIOR PERSPECTIVE STUDIES OF LIGHT AND SHADE; *OVERLEAF, L TO R*: EARLY INTERIOR STUDY; EARLY STUDY MODELS; *PAGE 46*: MODEL, PHASE V; *PAGE 47*: COMPUTER MONTAGE OF BUILDING IN SITE, PHASE VI

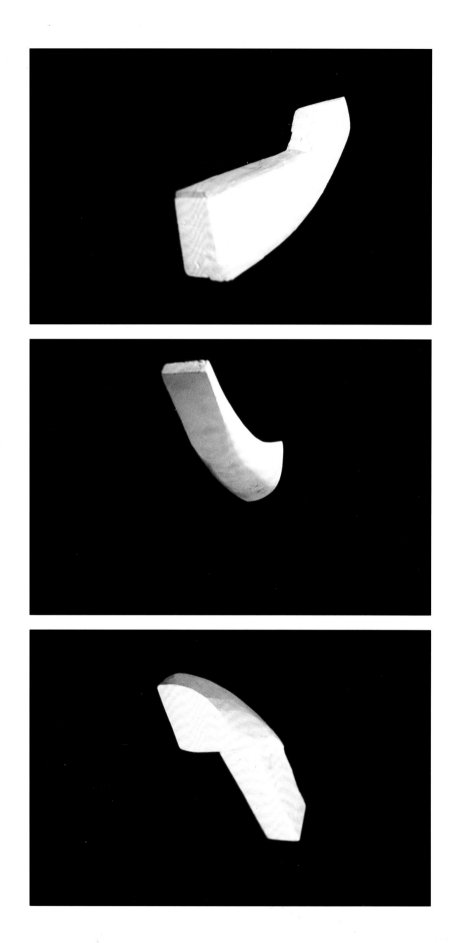

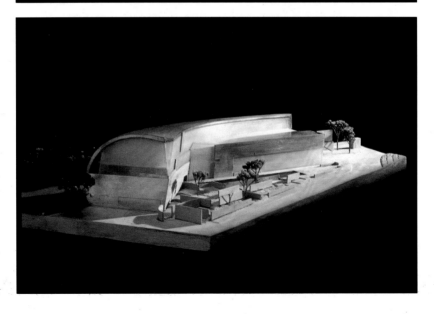

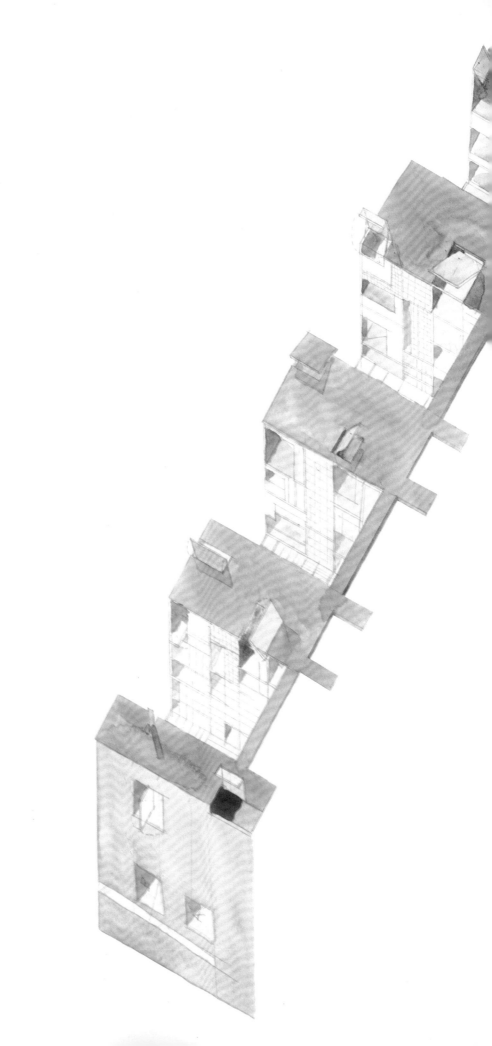

Steven Holl
Fukuoka Housing, Fukuoka, Japan

In the Fukuoka Housing project of 1991, four active north facing voids interlock with four quiet south-facing voids to bring a sense of the sacred into direct contact with everyday domestic life. To ensure emptiness, the south voids are flooded with water; the sun makes flickering reflections across the ceilings of the north courts and apartment interiors.

Interiors of the twenty-eight apartments revolve around the concept of 'hinged space', a development of the multi-use concepts of traditional Fusuma taken into an entirely modern dimension. One type of hinging (diurnal) allows an expansion of the living area during the day, reclaimed for bedrooms at night. Another type (episodic) reflects the change in a family over time: rooms can be added or subtracted to accommodate grown-up children leaving the family or elderly parents moving in.

An experiential sense of passage through space is heightened in the three types of access, which allow apartments to have exterior front doors. On the lower passage, views across the water court and through the north voids activate the walk spatially from side to side. Along the north passage one has a sense of suspension with the park in the distance. The top passage has a sky view under direct sunlight.

The apartments interlock in section like a complex Chinese box. Individuation from the standpoint of the individual inhabitant has an aim in making all twenty-eight apartments different. Due to the voids and interlocking section, each apartment has many exposures: north, south, east and west.

The structure of exposed bearing concrete is stained in some places. A lightweight aluminium curtain wall allows a reading of the building section while walking from east to west along the street; an entirely different facade of solids is exposed walking from west to east.

The building, with its street-aligned shops and intentionally simple facades, is seen as part of a city in its effort to form space rather than become an architecture of objects. Space is its medium from urban to private — hinged space.

WATERCOLOUR, CONCEPT SKETCH OF VOID AND HINGED SPACE HOUSING BLOCK; OVERLEAF: WATERCOLOUR OF VOID SPACE BRINGING A SACRED SPACE INTO THE EVERYDAY OF THE DOMESTIC BLOCK; OVERLEAF, FROM ABOVE RIGHT: WATERCOLOURS: HAKATA BAY, FUKUOKA — ORIGIN FOR 'WIND OF THE GODS' OR KAMIKAZE; STUDIES OF SINGLE AND DOUBLE LOADED COURTS; HINGED SPACE PLAN STUDY; STUDIES OF VOIDS

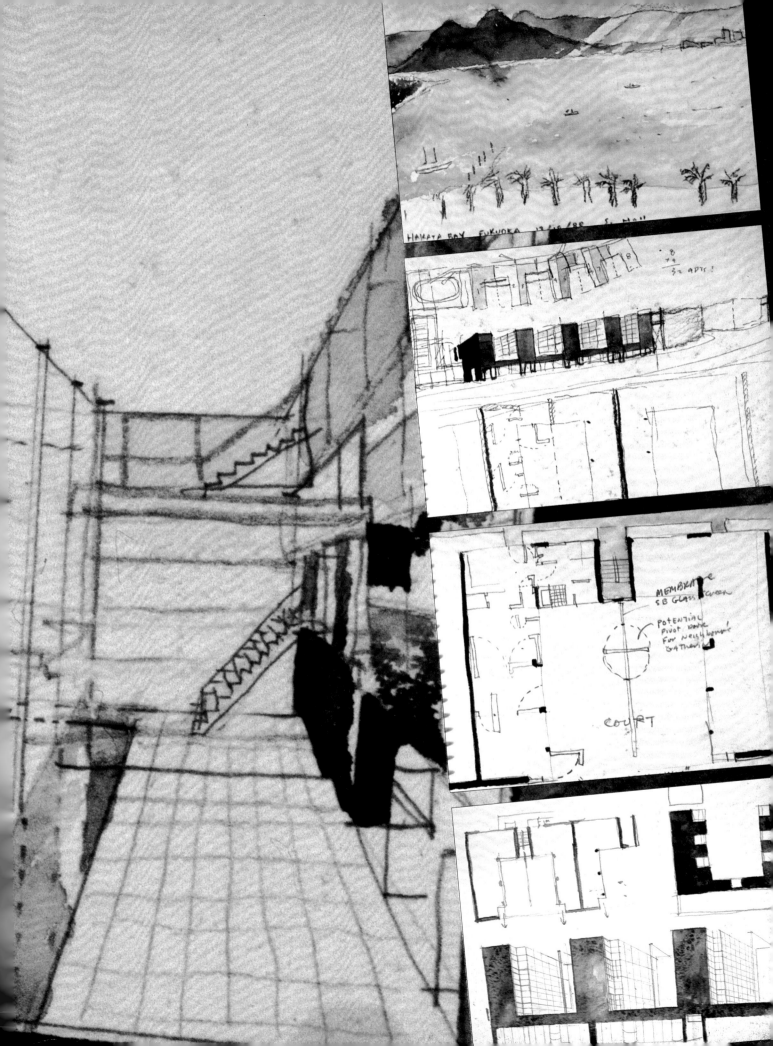

HAKATA BAY FUKUOKA 17/10/88 S. Holl

32 APTS!

MEMBRANE
SB GLASS SCREEN

POTENTIAL
PIVOT DOOR
FOR NEIGHBOR'S
GATHER

COURT

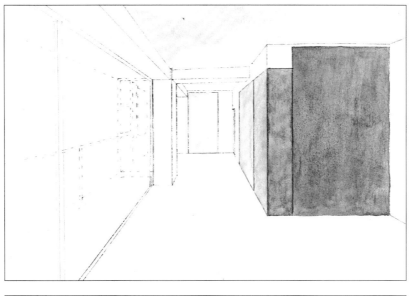

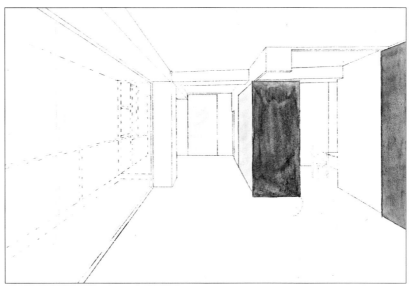

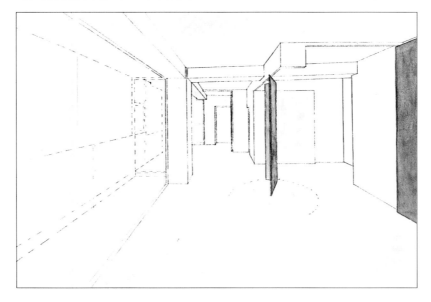

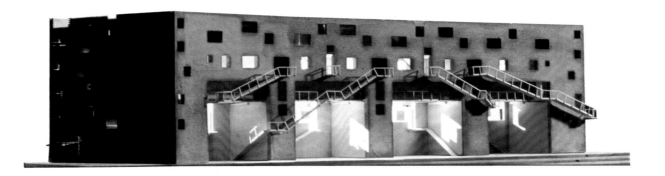

From Above: Front view of final built
project, 1989; model of north
elevation study for sun through the
block; *Previous Pages, L to R*:
Watercolour of water court passage;
hinged space watercolour studies –
opened and closed

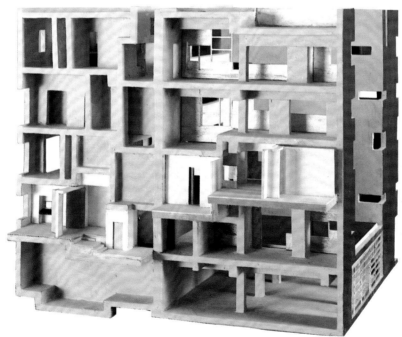

PARTIAL ELEVATION STUDY OF HEAVY
CONSTRUCTION VERSUS LIGHT AND
CURVILINEAR CONSTRUCTION; *OVERLEAF
LEFT*: WATERCOLOUR OF THE EXPLORATION
OF THE SITE'S EXISTING STREAM AND DAMS
WITH THE IDEA OF OVERHANGING ROOFS
AND OVERLAPPING SPACE; *OVERLEAF, FROM
ABOVE RIGHT*: WATERCOLOURS OF:
SHADOWS AND THE IDEA OF 'AQUEOUS
SPACE'; SUN AND SHADOWS EXPRESSED IN
AN EXPLORATION OF MASONRY, METAL
ROOFS AND TEXAS VERNACULAR ARCHITEC-
TURE; THE CONCEPT OF 'STRETTO' OR
OVERLAP WITH THE PARALLEL OF BELA
BARTOK'S MUSIC FOR STRINGS, PERCUSSION
AND CELESTE

Steven Holl
Texas Stretto House, Dallas, Texas

Sited adjacent to three spring-fed ponds with existing concrete dams, the house projects the character of the site in a series of concrete block 'spatial dams' with metal framed 'aqueous space' flowing through them. Flowing over the dams, like the overlapping stretto in music, water is an overlapping reflection of the landscape outside as well as the virtual overlapping of the space inside.

A particular music with this 'stretto', Bartók's *Music for Strings, Percussion and Celeste* was a parallel on which the house form was made. In four movements, the piece has a distinct division between heavy (percussion) and light (strings). Where music has a materiality in instrumentation and sound, this architecture attempts an analogue in light and space, that is:

$$\frac{material \times sound}{time} = \frac{material \times light}{space}$$

The building is formed in four parts, each consisting of two modes: firstly, heavy orthogonal masonry and secondly, light and curvilinear metal. The plan is purely orthogonal; the section curvilinear. The guest house is an inversion with the plan curvilinear and the section orthogonal, similar to the inversions of the subject in the first movement of the Bartók score. In the main house aqueous space is developed by several means: floor planes pull the level of one space through to the next, roof planes pull space over walls and an arched wall pulls light down from a skylight. Materials and details continue the spatial concepts in poured concrete, cast glass in fluid shapes, slumped glass and terrazzo. Arriving via a driveway bridging the stream, one passes through overlapping spaces of the house, glimpsing the gardens and arriving at an empty room flooded by the pond. The room, doubling its space in reflection, becomes the asymmetrical centre of two sequences of aqueous space arriving finally at an empty flooded room.

CHANCE
2. ORDERING 45%

SUSTAINED
"MATHEMATICAL
ORDERING
55%"

SPACE
LIGHT
3.

BETWEEN

FIELD
SPACE
ENTIRE

BRIDGE

GUEST
HOUSE

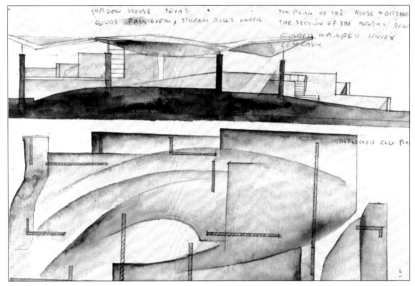

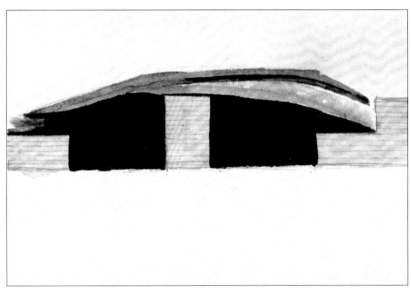

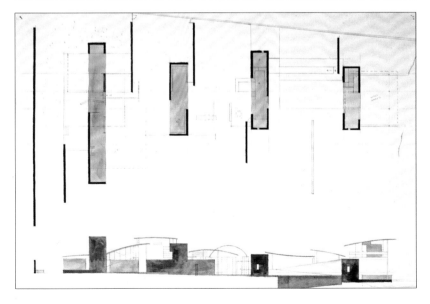

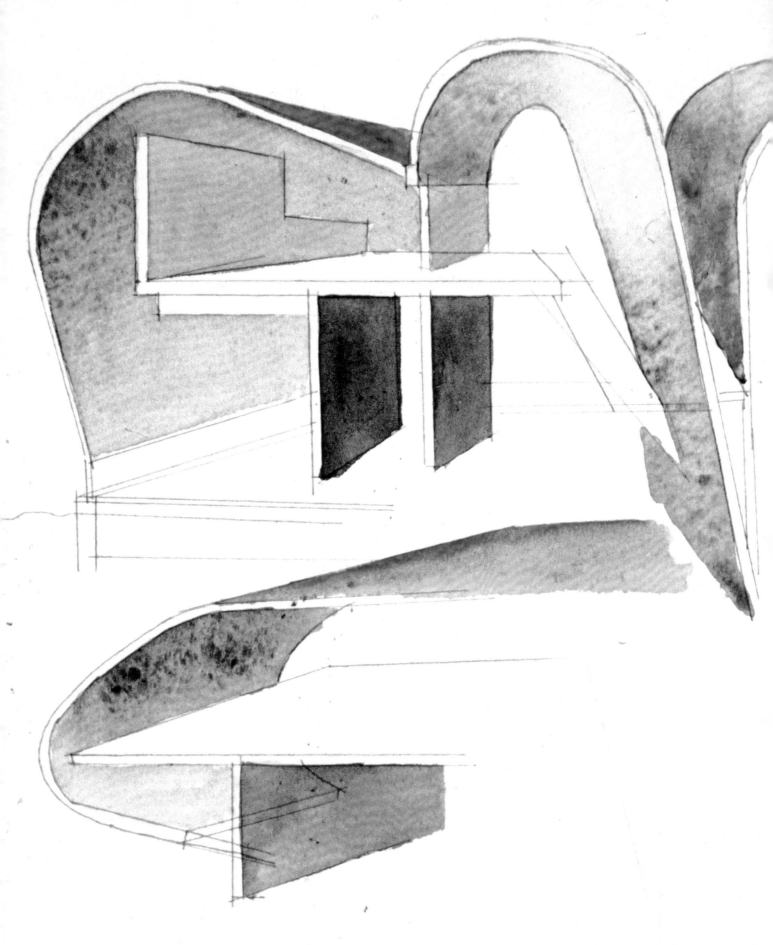

TEXAS Stretto

S. Holl

WATERCOLOUR, INTERIOR STUDY OF
OVERLAPPING 'AQUEOUS' SPACE; *OPPOSITE*:
WATERCOLOUR, FIRST SKETCH OF CONCEPT
OF SPACE ANALOGOUS TO MUSICAL OVERLAP
OR 'STRETTO'

FINAL MODEL, VIEW TO WEST; *OPPOSITE*:
WATERCOLOUR, FLOODED ROOM – THE
CENTRE OF THE SITE AND HOUSE
COMPOSITION

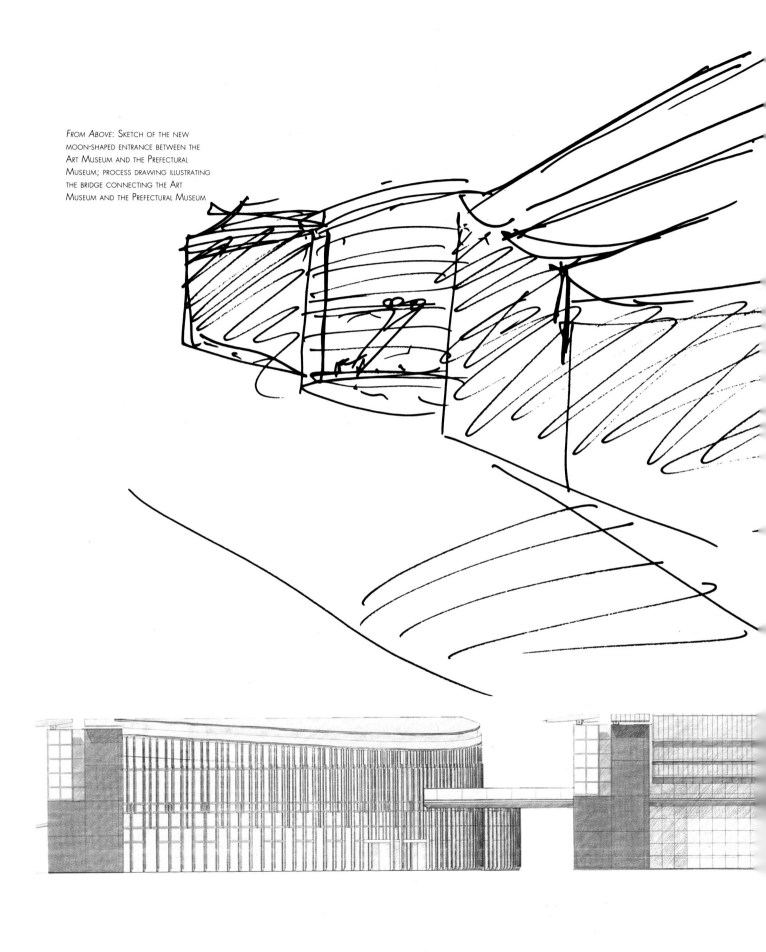

FROM ABOVE: SKETCH OF THE NEW
MOON-SHAPED ENTRANCE BETWEEN THE
ART MUSEUM AND THE PREFECTURAL
MUSEUM; PROCESS DRAWING ILLUSTRATING
THE BRIDGE CONNECTING THE ART
MUSEUM AND THE PREFECTURAL MUSEUM

Kisho Kurokawa
Wakayama Prefectural Museum, the Museum of Modern Art, Wakayama, Japan

Symbiosis with Nature

The site is located on what used to be a part of the ancient Wakayama Castle grounds, and at present this area is divided into two with a road running in between. The other divided area would become a park and eventually be connected by a wide pedestrian walkway over the road. Pans to construct the Wakayama Prefectural Museum and Museum of Modern Art were proposed after the university, which formerly occupied the site, had relocated.

Symbiosis with History

Castle architecture in Japan was first developed in the fifteenth, sixteenth and seventeenth centuries. The design of the roof and the eaves is symbolic of these eras. The museum expresses the symbiosis of the history and the present by referring to traditional eaves but in an abstract way.

The colours proposed here would be black and white, also quoted from the traditional castle architecture style.

The Art Museum and the Prefectural Museum are designed with simple geometric forms. Furthermore, the geometric form of the entrance hall is abstracted from a crescent. To show the identity of each building and to create a dramatic interrelation, the exterior finishes of the Art Museum are proposed in black ceramic tile, while those of the Prefectural Museum proposed in white ceramic tile.

The arrangement of architecture and its forms is carefully designed to evade symmetry. The edge of the pond, where the architecture is situated, is designed in linear fashion, and the park side is designed with natural curved lines so as to express the traditional Japanese culture of asymmetry.

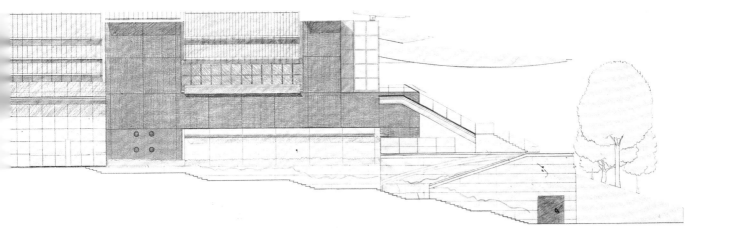

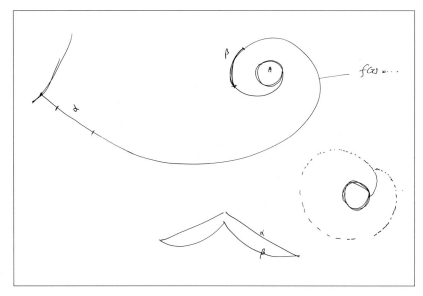

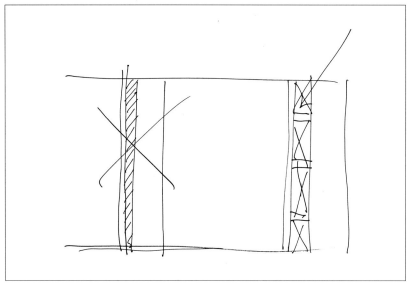

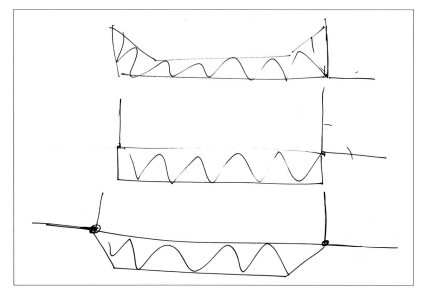

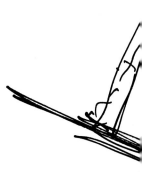

FROM ABOVE: SKETCH OF DISPLAY BOARD
ON THE WALL; SELF STANDING DISPLAY
BOARD; *OPPOSITE, FROM ABOVE:* SKETCH
ILLUSTRATING THE USE OF THE MODERN
CROSSOID AND FRACTAL CURVES FOR DETAIL;
STUDY SKETCH EXPLORING THE USE OF THE
TRUSSES FOR THE GLASS FACADE STUD;
VARIOUS SKETCHES ILLUSTRATING BRIDGES
CONNECTING THE ART MUSEUM AND THE
PREFECTURAL MUSEUM

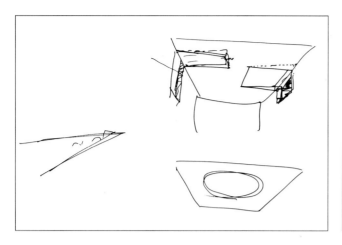

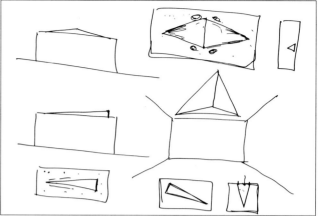

From Above: Design sketches of indirect light fittings for the ceiling; roof forms – studies of the wall material

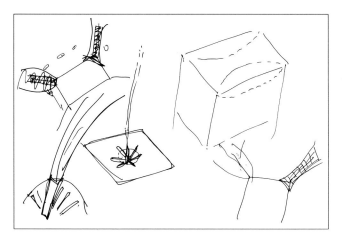

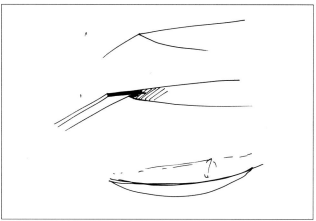

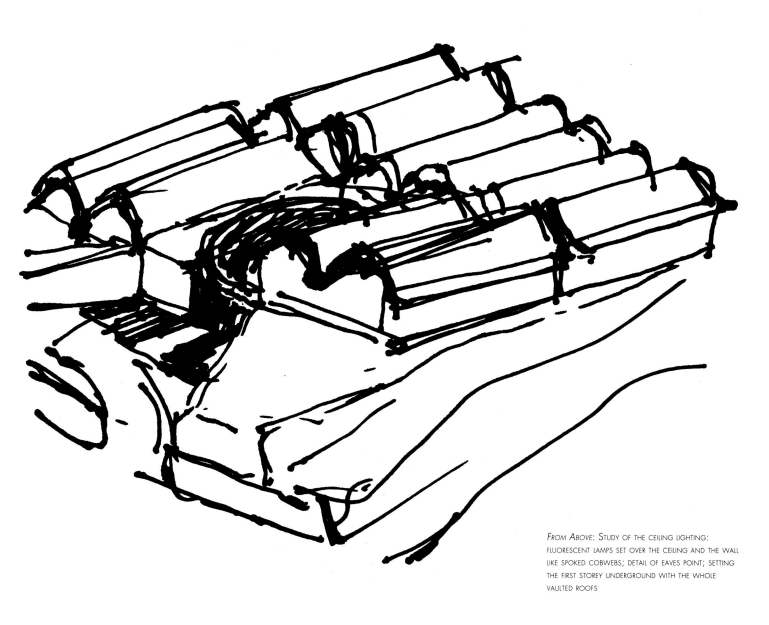

From Above: Study of the ceiling lighting: fluorescent lamps set over the ceiling and the wall like spoked cobwebs; detail of eaves point; setting the first storey underground with the whole vaulted roofs

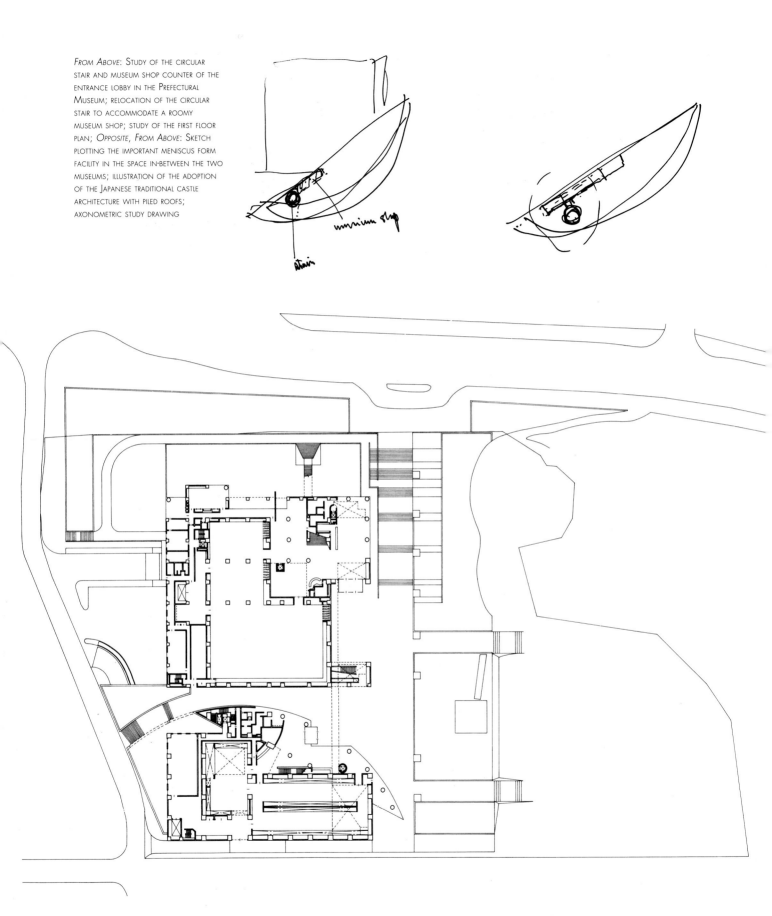

From Above: Study of the circular
stair and museum shop counter of the
entrance lobby in the Prefectural
Museum; relocation of the circular
stair to accommodate a roomy
museum shop; study of the first floor
plan; *Opposite, From Above*: Sketch
plotting the important meniscus form
facility in the space in-between the two
museums; illustration of the adoption
of the Japanese traditional castle
architecture with piled roofs;
axonometric study drawing

museum shop

stair

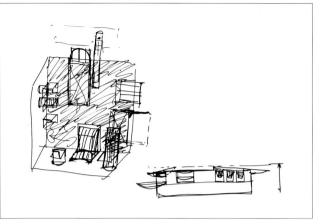

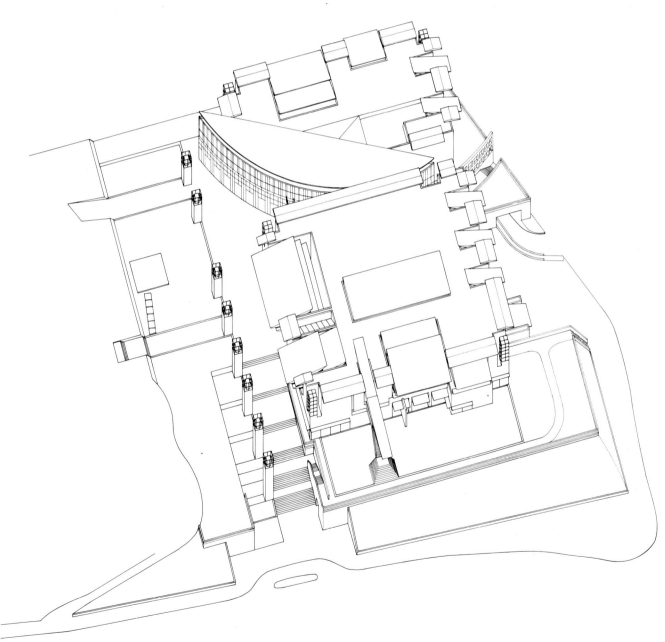

STUDY DRAWING OF THE ENTRANCE LOBBY OF THE PREFECTURAL MUSEUM

STUDY OF THE ATRIUM OF THE ENTRANCE LOBBY AND MEZZANINE FLOOR

SECTIONAL STUDY DRAWING OF THE ENTRANCE LOBBY OF THE PREFECTURAL MUSEUM

TERRACE OF THE ADMINISTRATION BUILDING — STUDY OF THE LAYOUT OF THE FURNITURE

STUDY MODEL

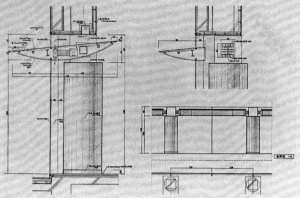

Detailed study of the eaves of the facade of the Art Museum

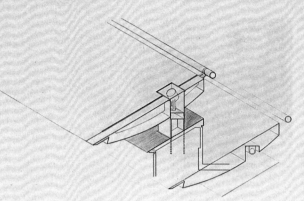

Top beam and handrail of the rising part of the terrace

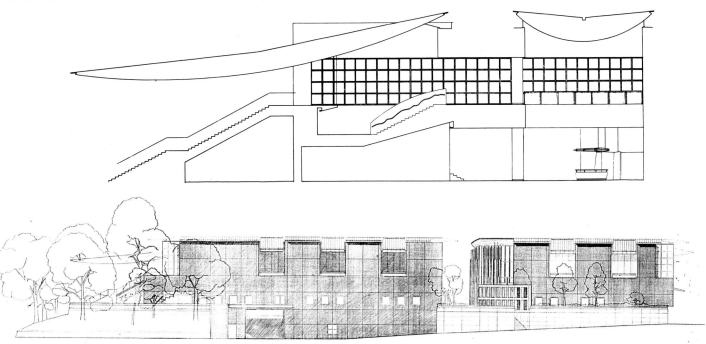

From Above: Study model; sectional
sketch of the canopy over the
restaurant entrance; east elevation

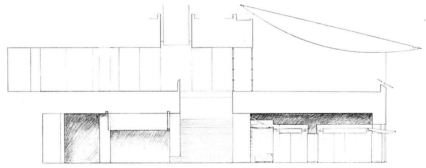

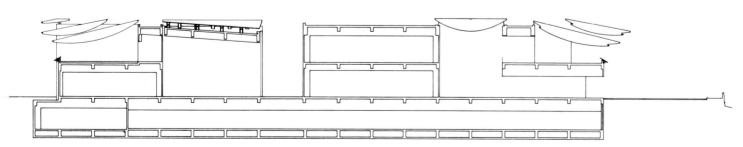

FROM ABOVE: VIEW OF THE ART MUSEUM
AND THE PREFECTURAL MUSEUM FROM THE
MAIN APPROACH; SECTIONAL DRAWINGS OF
THE TERRACE AND EAVES AND ART MUSEUM

Morphosis
Salick Healthcare Office Building,
Beverly Hills, Los Angeles

The challenge of creating a public presence through the formal and pragmatic transfiguration of an existing building became the departure point for the Salick Healthcare Office Building. The site was essentially read as one of three dimensions, since the brief required the transformation of the nondescript, neutral existing office building which occupied it. Onto this generic, prototypically LA urban site came the commission to develop a possibly even more prosaic structure. The architects' initial instinct was to challenge the generic by creating a more differential entity to replace it.

The strategy concentrates on identifying and resolving a series of existing formal conditions, including an emphasis on the expression of the corner site condition, an engagement of the awkwardly-placed mechanical penthouse volume and a discrimination of the facades. In the place of the undifferentiated box of horizontal slabs which existed prior to this intervention, a series of vertically oriented components, opaque and transparent, was positioned which essentially functions to divide the formerly monolithic structure into two separate buildings.

Each facade was addressed to minimise or maximise solar heat gain, producing extremes of opacity on the south and west, which contrasts with the transparency of the east and north. The east facade reveals the irregular nature of the existing steel frame which is used as a datum for the new envelope. Previously undifferentiated aspects, including the upper and lower segments of entry, the corner condition, the roof boundary and various day/night lighting conditions were seen as opportunities to express the integration of discrete parts and were seen as analogous to, and mimetic of, patterns of accretional urban growth.

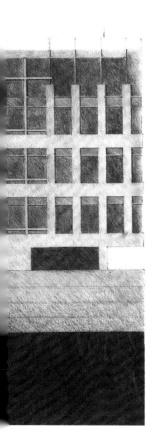

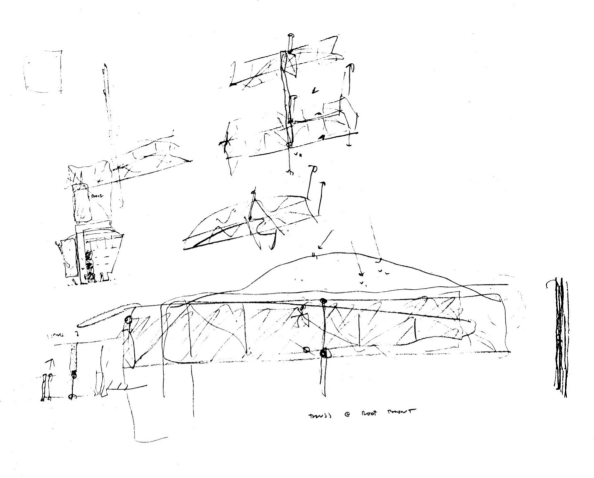

truss @ roof front

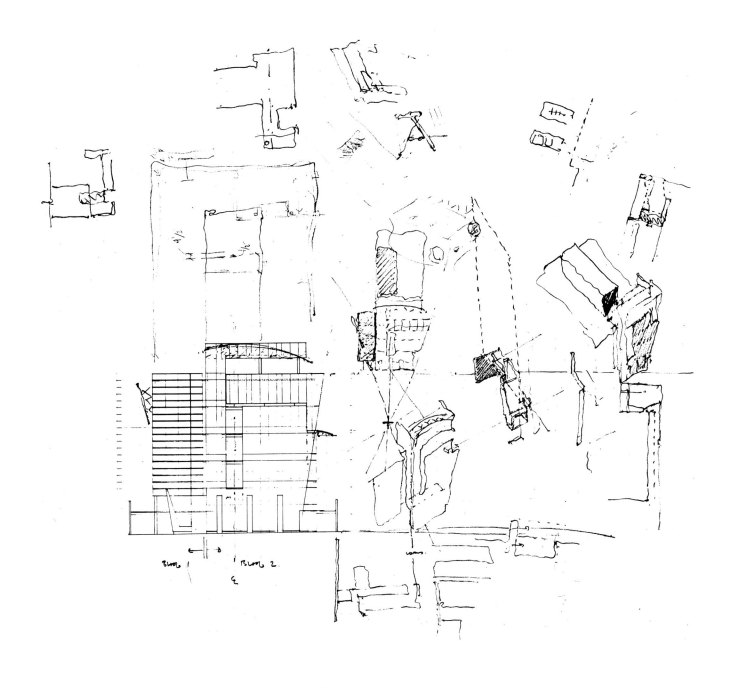

BLDG 1   BLDG 2.

SECTION WITH DETAILS; *OPPOSITE, FROM
ABOVE:* PRELIMINARY SKETCHES OF THE
ROOF TRUSS; SECTIONAL SKETCH

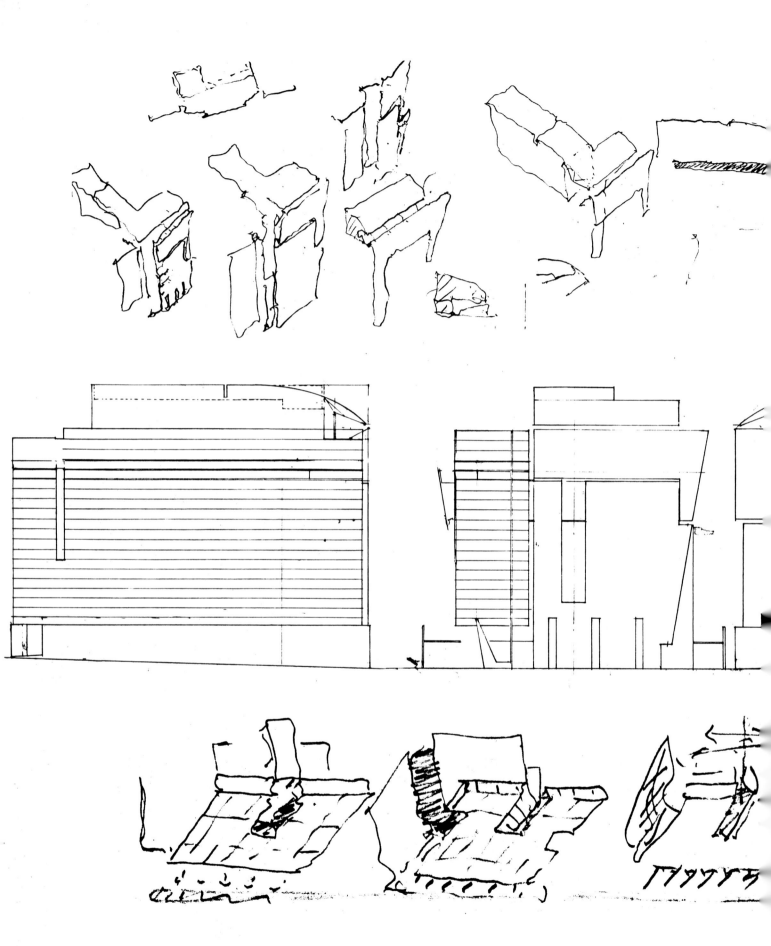

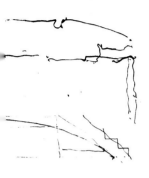

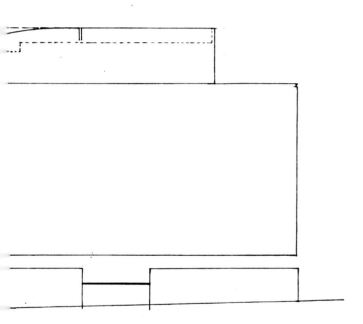

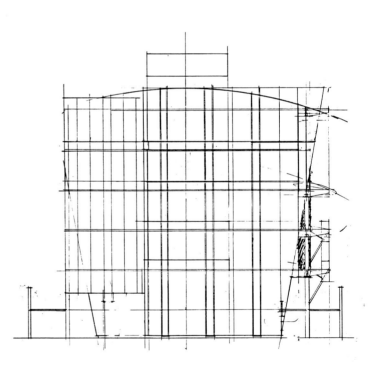

FROM ABOVE: DEVELOPMENTAL SKETCHES IN
SEQUENCE WITH EARLY ELEVATIONS AND
DETAILS

L TO R: PHOTOGRAPHIC MONTAGE OF
RESIDENCE UNDER CONSTRUCTION;
PRELIMINARY SKETCHES

Morphosis
Blades Residence, Santa Barbara, California

A large exterior room has been created within which the house is situated. This room embraces an augmented natural landscape conveying a sense of sanctuary. Experientially, this strategy provides an opportunity for the occupant to witness the enigmatic interactions of nature; one is made aware of the value of diversity and difference. This perception of integration allows one to cope with the haphazardness of complex life. Through the fusion of the exterior and interior worlds, the individual gradually becomes oriented . . . learns to keep one's balance. This interaction aspires to bridge the gap between the subjective experience of one's inner world and the objective experience of one's outer world.

The building arrangement, while alluding to the specific characteristics of this site, ultimately demonstrates its tentativeness to fixity by making overt reference to our temporary status as occupants. The work is a manifestation of an organisational strategy capable of representing a high degree of differentiation within a framework of order and continuity. The complex of pieces expresses states of both harmony and tension in the sense that this co-existence of difference (between the wilful architectural elements and the augmented landscape) is inherently conflictive. These architectural landscape elements confront, but are simultaneously at home with, the untouched grounds. The fractured characteristic of the solution provides a perpetual open-endedness and unfinished quality to the project. It is part of an accretive making process that anticipates the next intervention.

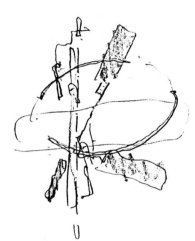

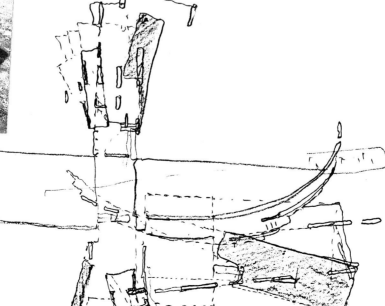

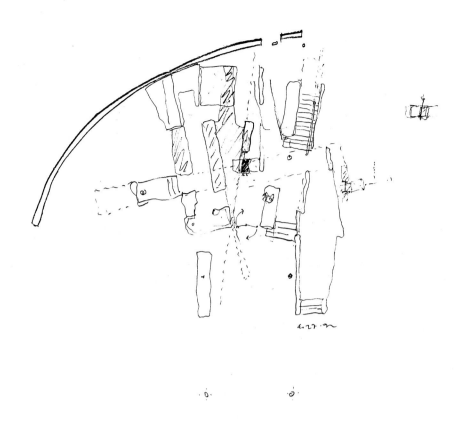

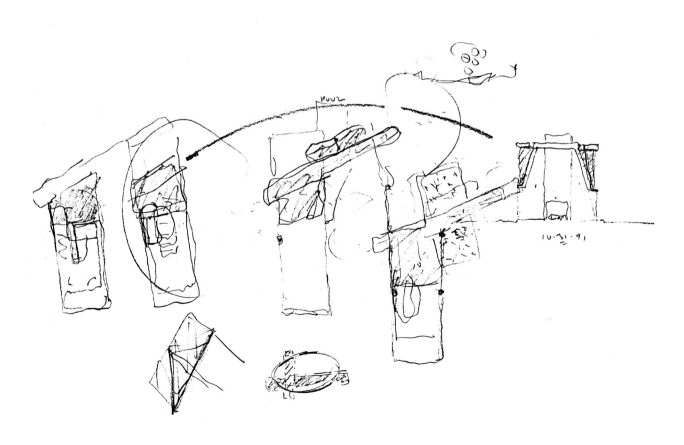

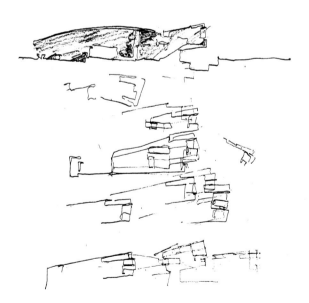

Developmental sketches in sequence

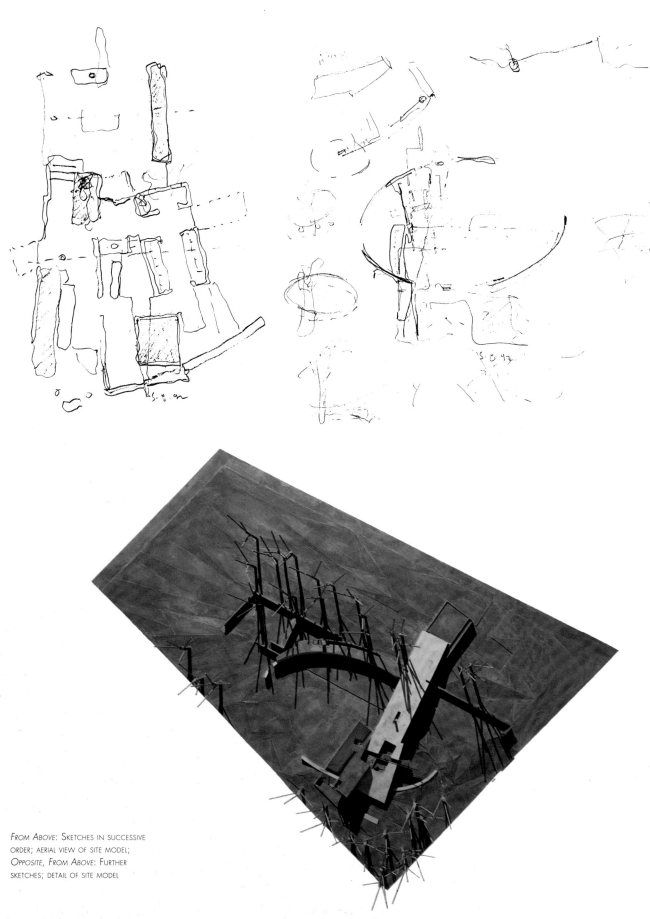

FROM ABOVE: SKETCHES IN SUCCESSIVE
ORDER; AERIAL VIEW OF SITE MODEL;
OPPOSITE, FROM ABOVE: FURTHER
SKETCHES; DETAIL OF SITE MODEL

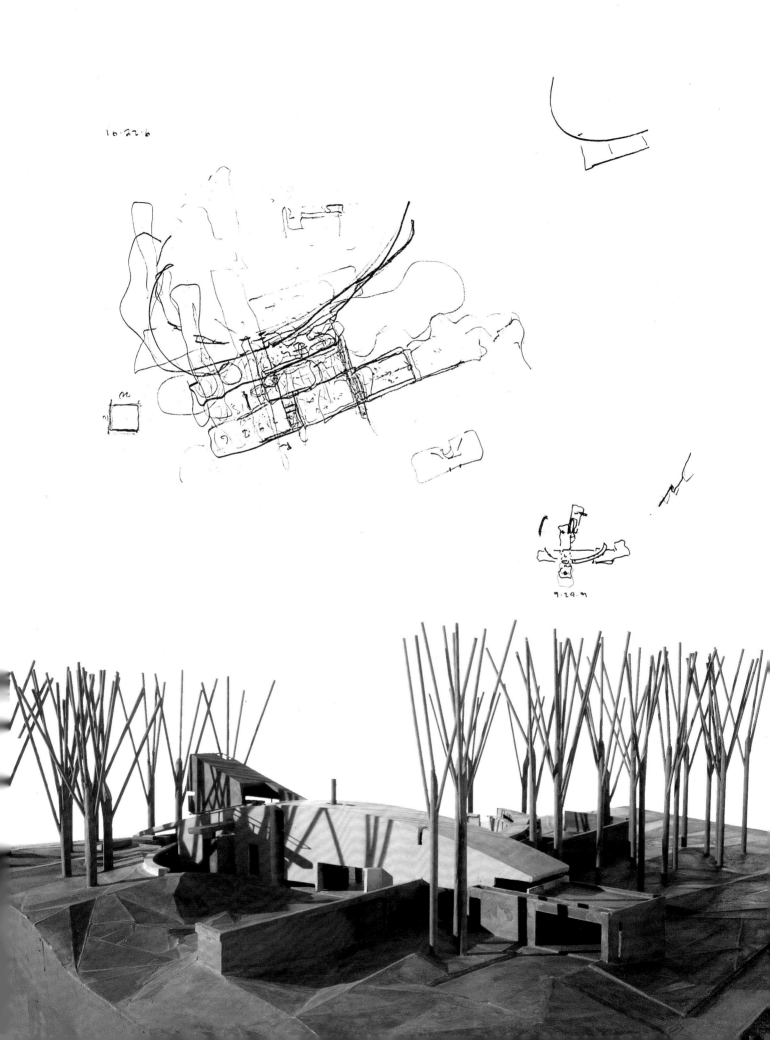

Morphosis
Diamond Ranch High School, Pomona, Los Angeles

The proposal focuses on three major areas. The first is the architects' desire to take advantage of the natural beauty of the site by integrating the playing fields and the buildings into the surrounding hillside. The second goal was to create a dynamic built environment which would foster maximum interaction between students, teachers, administration and the community. Finally, the proposal attempts to facilitate a flexible teaching environment that allows a solid foundation of core curriculum for grades 9-10 and offers the opportunity for students to focus on specific programme majors in grades 11-12.

The proposal employs a modified, stepped, grading plan, which reflects the slope of the hillside. There is a total of thirty-six usable acres (twenty-five of which are used for various playing fields). It is the intent that the 'building becomes site' and that the 'site becomes building', illustrating an idea of the integration of nature and environment.

One of the major focal points of the scheme is an open amphitheatre that allows movement from the main school areas to the roof terrace and football field above, while creating a student gathering area. It also serves as an outdoor theatre for the performing arts classroom – the exterior wall lifts and transforms this drama space to a stage.

The majority of the playing fields are located to the north and west of the site. A pedestrian walkway/emergency vehicle assess-way connects the fields to the school and creates a natural slope for the viewing of baseball games. The primary football field is embedded into the hill at the south of the site to create an economical seating area. The gymnasium, to the east, mimics the hillside with a pitched roof which undulates with the terrain. The parking areas are a formal extension of the gymnasium, fanning outward and stepping up the hillside.

From the east entry road, one is greeted by a curved wall which denotes entry. The administration building, which is conceived as an extension of the entry sequence, is a gateway and control point to the school. The first contains general administrative activities with student services on the second floor. Past the administration building, the school opens up to form a 'pedestrian street'. This pedestrian system is the primary connecting link of the school interlinking all academic, ancillary and support, and social and meeting spaces. An elevated walkway parallels this pedestrian way and forms its northern edge, connecting the 9-10 grade clusters, the library and the administration. The library, which is adjacent to the administration, is located on two floors with individual computer study cubicles above. It forms an 'information bridge' formally connecting the north and south buildings of the school.

The gymnasium controls access from the parking to the stadium field. The back wall of the gymnasium is a repetitive 'buttress retaining wall'. These buttresses penetrate the roof terrace plane offering the opportunity to support shading devices and flexible seating for the stadium. The main dining facilities adjacent to the gymnasium are open to natural sunlight and ventilation, being organised around a large two-storey volume. Its location is appropriate to its use with access to a north facing court at the main pedestrian and the terrace above. Possibly the most compelling public gathering space will be this rooftop terrace at the level of the football stadium offering a panoramic view of the school, the playing fields and the city beyond.

The 9-10 grade clusters are located to the north side of the 'pedestrian street'. These are conceived as small 'schools within the school' and are articulated by separate two-storey buildings which create a total of six clusters. Each cluster has its own outdoor gathering space, teacher's workroom and guidance area, with the classrooms wrapping around the centre creating outdoor areas between with views of the valley beyond. The classrooms are equipped with movable partitions which allow flexibility. Although the clusters are separate entities, they open up to the pedestrian street and they are arranged in a split-level configuration maximising access with stairs and ramps. An

open space is left to the east for future expansion.

The bulk of the classrooms for grades 11-12 are positioned to the south of the street and are arranged around open air courtyards. The majority of the core curriculum classrooms are grouped around two courtyards on the second level, with shared computer labs and teachers' workrooms integrated around these cores. The more specific curriculum areas (eg industrial technology) and the student centre is located on the first floor. The amphitheatre forms a link to the east with the performing arts labs and dining facilities. Use of the roof is made by the connection of the amphitheatre and acts as another student gathering/ outdoor area. The building acts as a retaining wall to the hillside while using a series of repetitive 'buttress walls' to facilitate an economical system.

It was the architects' intent to create a building which is perceived as at one with the site. By incorporating the topography with outdoor playing fields, public spaces and rooftops, the architects have attempted to create a cohesive environment between building and landscape. In a similar manner, the building is also integrated with its users through the use of courtyards and a pedestrian street which encourages integration while fostering a flexible learning community. This project accommodates the educational programme and simultaneously demonstrates, in a tangible way, a means of negotiating a method of preserving nature.

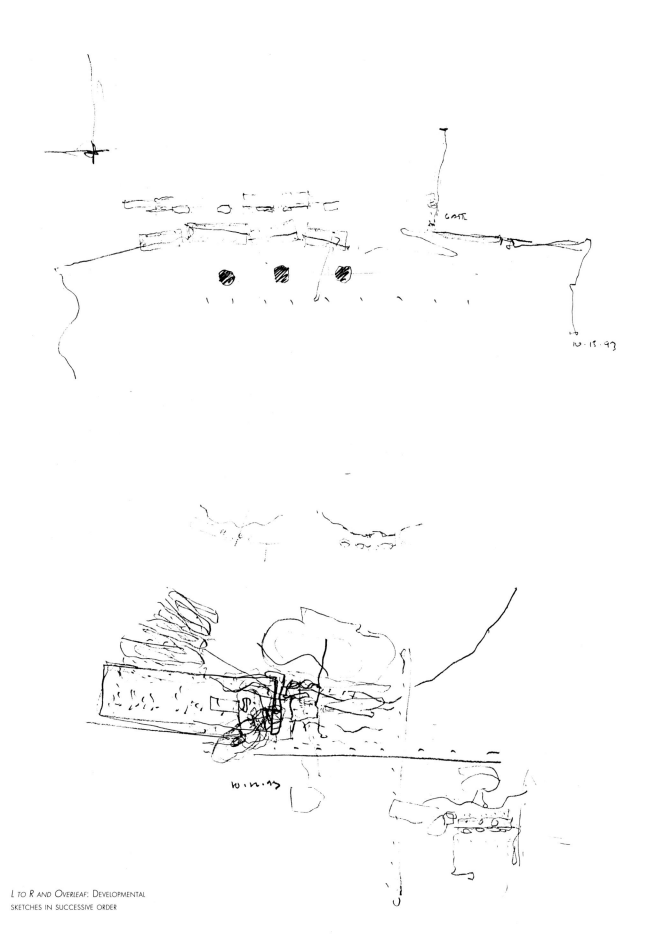

L to R and Overleaf: Developmental
sketches in successive order

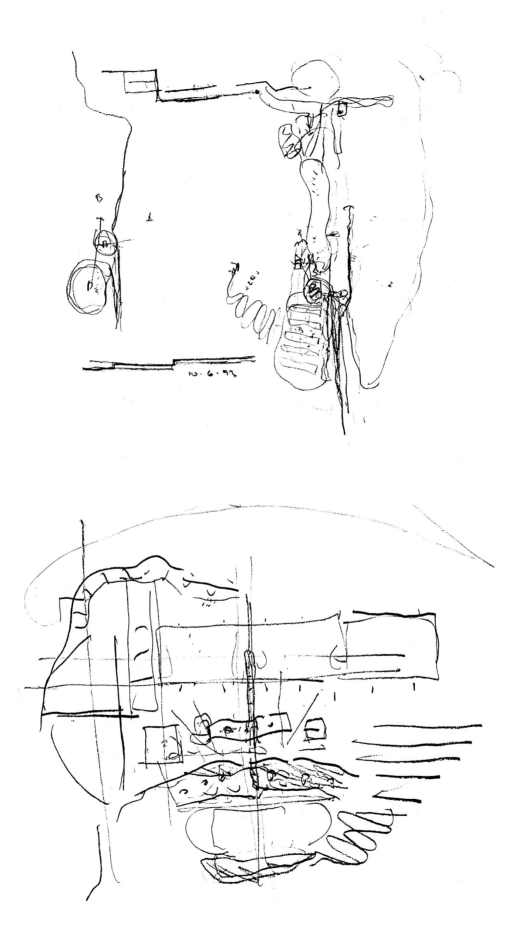

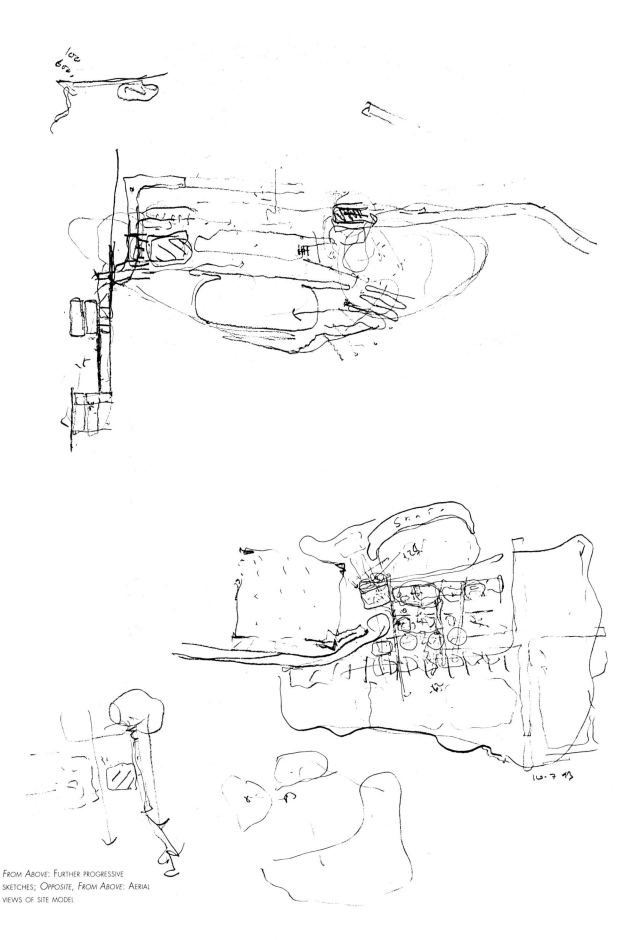

From Above: Further progressive sketches; Opposite, From Above: Aerial views of site model

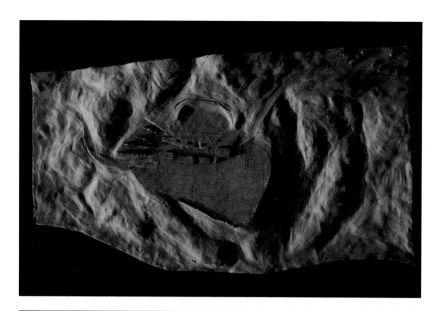

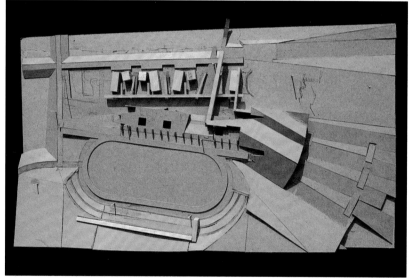

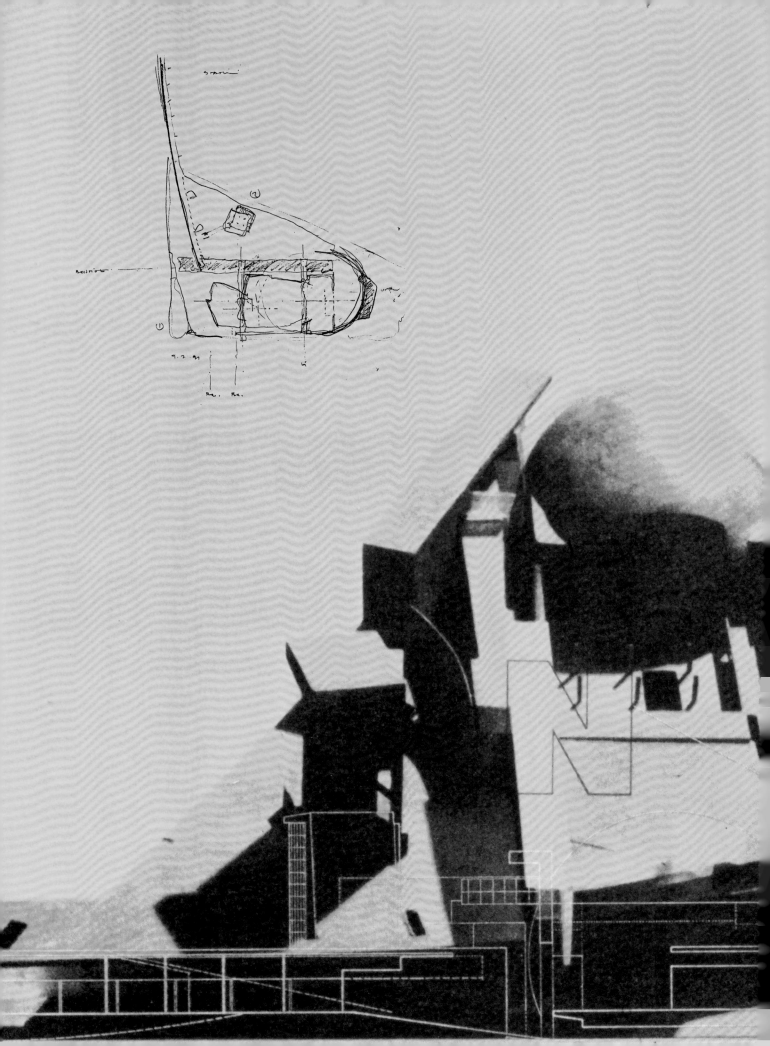

Morphosis

Nara Convention Hall, Nara, Japan

The city of Tokyo has been described as the 'city of unattainable voids' by Barthes. In Nara, as in Tokyo, palaces and other sacred spaces occupy epicentres in the city. Movement becomes a matter of circumventing these boundaries. The solution to the Nara competition began as an edge fragment of a conceptual void, an inhabitable place, intended to be read as a connective device which designates a boundary, creates a mark. A tilted plane reconfigures the site like a tectonic plate, bridging the railroad and the centre of the city to this site, and acting as a datum for the three theatres that are the main elements of the project. The egg-shaped two-thousand-seat theatre stands in juxtaposition to the diverse, day-to-day texture of the city. In contrast to the openness of the Black Box, this massive form – opaque, polished and enigmatic – conceals its interior world. One can sense that these are but the beginnings in a series of more complex organisations. The egg metaphor is enclosed, internal, and mysterious yet evocative of the sublime beauty to be found in one of nature's most fundamental objects. It is a metaphor of Nara's traditional importance in the formation of a national world view, as well as the embryonic potential that this centre has as a point of departure for future redevelopment.

In contrast to this mysterious, protective form, the Black Box is transparent, acting as a classical object and as an apparatus isolated in open space. This hundred-seat theatre is dynamic rather than static, with a mechanised floor that allows for multiple staging configurations. The Recital Hall, which is the third major element, negotiates between the sloping plane of the public space and the curving connective bridge, with a glass wall that acts as a marquee and gateway to the city. An interior street, which is actually a conceptual void, connects these three halls and is a continuation of the urban street grid, documenting the structure of the city and its historical roots. It is mimetic of it in the way that various programmatic elements, such as galleries and restaurants, connect to it.

The main idea of the referential perimeter was seen to be a connecting device to the city. It embraces and is place-making rather than axial as in the Arts Park Project. It is at once contingent and platonic, passive and aggressive in its approach to dealing with contextual issues. In terms of its approach to the city, Nara represents a middle ground between the relatively compliant solution for the Berlin Library and the more aggressive approach in Vienna. There is a consciously controlled hierarchic clarity of position which pays direct homage to Stirling with respect to his sequential investigations in Cologne, Düsseldorf, and the Stuttgart Staatsgalerie.

OPPOSITE, FROM ABOVE: PRELIMINARY SKETCH; MONTAGE OF NORTH ELEVATION WITH PLAN OVERLAID

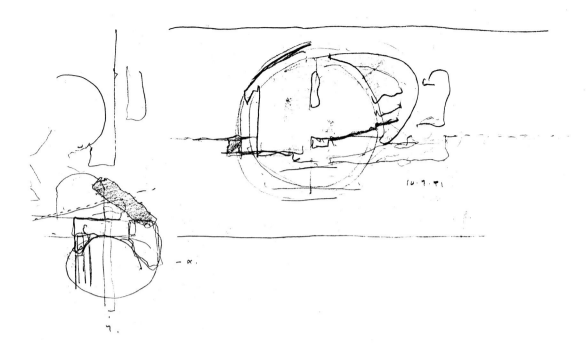

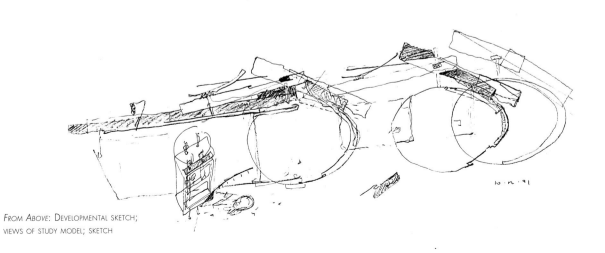

FROM ABOVE: DEVELOPMENTAL SKETCH;
VIEWS OF STUDY MODEL; SKETCH

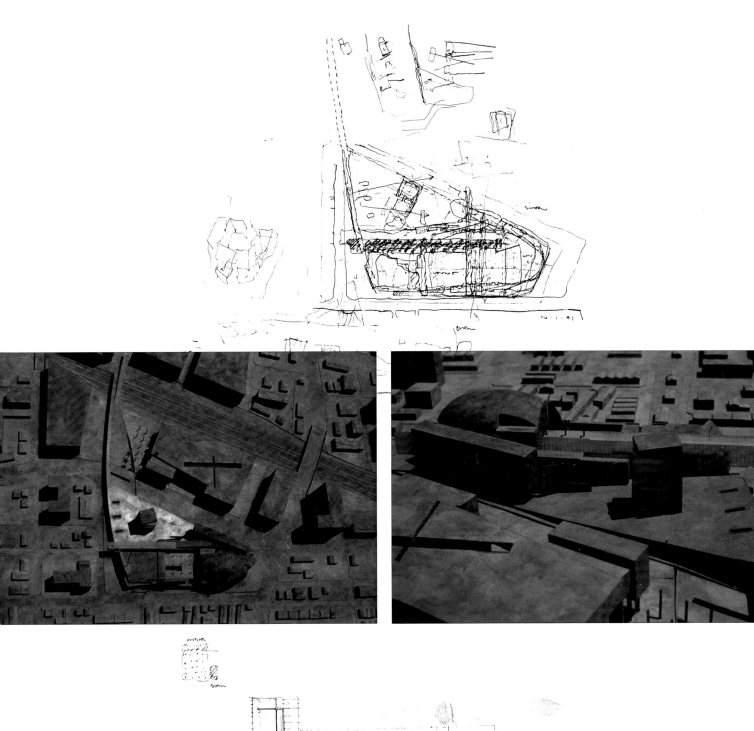

FROM ABOVE: FURTHER PROGRESSIVE
SKETCH; VIEWS OF STUDY MODEL; SECTIONAL
SKETCH

Morphosis
Tours Competition, Tours, France

The project produces a spatial configuration which defines an interior courtyard space and implies a symmetrical relationship between the dramatic arts and the visual arts. The architects chose to respect the qualities and the atmosphere made by musical instruments. These sounds, perceived in an enclosed courtyard, create a peaceful place for the contemplation of a fragment of music, a nuance of wind sounds. With the new intervention, the plastic arts will now be fully integrated in this tranquil space by being glimpsed through the walls of the CCC or in the courtyard itself as sculpture.

The new square will be the site's focal point of student activities where special events could be created, such as an outdoor theatre connected to the new stage or music concerts or eventually plastic intervention connected to the gallery.

The scale of the project provides an opportunity to create an intervention which will give the site a complete coherence and reveal its potential to the town. The solution does not rest on the addition of a single space, rather it relies on the addition of a series of spaces which recomposes a sequence of spatial events as one travels through the site. This approach is attentive to the need for the preservation of the existing pedagogic activities during construction at different stages. The architects chose to augment the value of the existing architecture as a departure point for the project. The existing facades, the general massing and the Chapel's apse are all integrated as a series of public spaces which are perceived by moving through the site.

The recreation of the edge-wall facade facing Rue du Petit Prés forms the boundary of the foyer space for the theatre and intensifies the pedestrian/automobile connection to the foyer from the town. The theatre sector of the proposal is intentionally dense and compresses against this boundary. One enters through a gate in this wall into the theatre which is on axis to the main pedestrian connection.

The north side of the site is accessed through the creation of a small plaza redefining the Church's apse and is the threshold space before entering the CCC. There will be gates at each of these boundaries which will allow for security for all parts of the complex.

A pedestrian path was created to connect all main building functions within the complex. One enters this interior pathway through a portal in the wall at the theatre's edge or at the interior boundary of the threshold park to the North. Alternatively one arrives from the lower level parking which provides access to the courtyard at a point equidistant between the CCC and the Theatre. From this midpoint one is immediately immersed in an active environment within sight of the cafe. Particular attention was given to the creation of these pedestrian paths to create animated spaces able to be a kind of promenade architecturale through both the site and through the inside of the buildings. This path can also be used as access/egress for fire trucks.

If new pedagogic needs were to occur, the site plan permits the insertion of a new building between Paul Courrier High School and the Rue du Petit Prés in symmetry with the new CNR.

The main objective was to concentrate the CNR programmes in continuity with the existing building and to connect it to one single area with the theatre administration. According to phasing and budget it was decided to limit the interventions in the existing building. This strategy presents several advantages: interventions can be made during vacations without the cessation of teaching; and both additions will be independent phases which are connected at the conclusion of the second phase. Both phases are anticipated to meet budget constraints.

The CCC was conceived as a theatre of sorts, a backdrop or a stage for the artwork that it exhibits. A 'neutral' space has been produced, not Cartesian or Euclidean, but a space which defines its neutrality by adopting the mid-level structure of the site, utilising the configuration of the curved wall. The gallery space is uniformly lit with reflected south-facing light. The shape of the space allows for multiple configurations responding to the requirement for myriad discrete, isolated venues. A series of idiosyncratic, small openings gives clues to the exterior environment (Breuer's Whitney NYC). These enclosures can be closed for certain types of exhibits, and a low, transparent wall parallels the exterior sculpture court which allows for interior/exterior programmatic possibilities. This wall, too, can be closed, based on the requirements of the exhibit. The entry is at the interstitial point between the newly created public plaza at the church and the interior court adjacent to the cafe, which becomes the main public space of the Creation Center.

The configuration and the development of the theatre is the result of its compressed condition between the interior court and the street. This situation is best understood by the configuration of the foyer space which articulates a vertical space documenting the extremes of the subterranean and the sky. One moves along the edges of this unoccupiable space which serves the foyer activities for the theatre. The house floor and the balcony configuration is a continued expression of this compression and produces a house space roughly equal in size to the stage dimensions. Ancillary activities, stage assembly, green rooms, administrative offices, etc, are located on three floors parallel to the theatre and the pedestrian access way.

The scheme respects the phasing scheme as stipulated in the programme, as phasing allows for minimal disturbance of teaching activities.

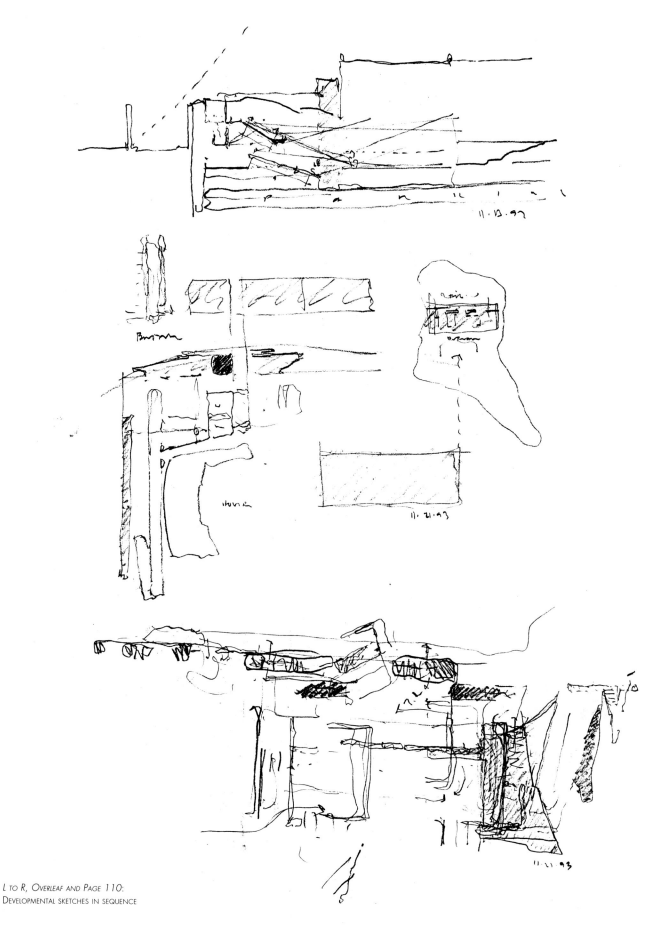

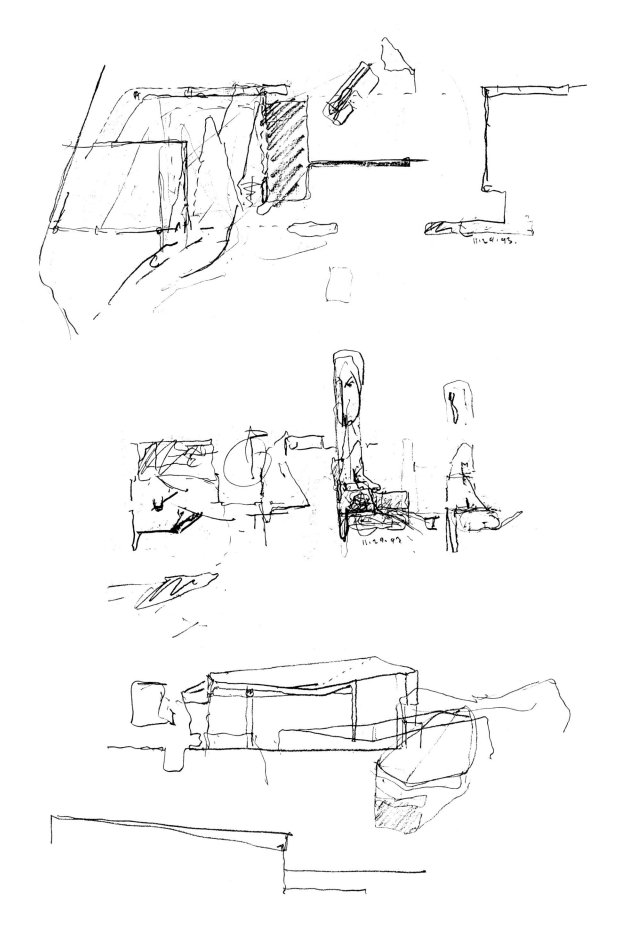

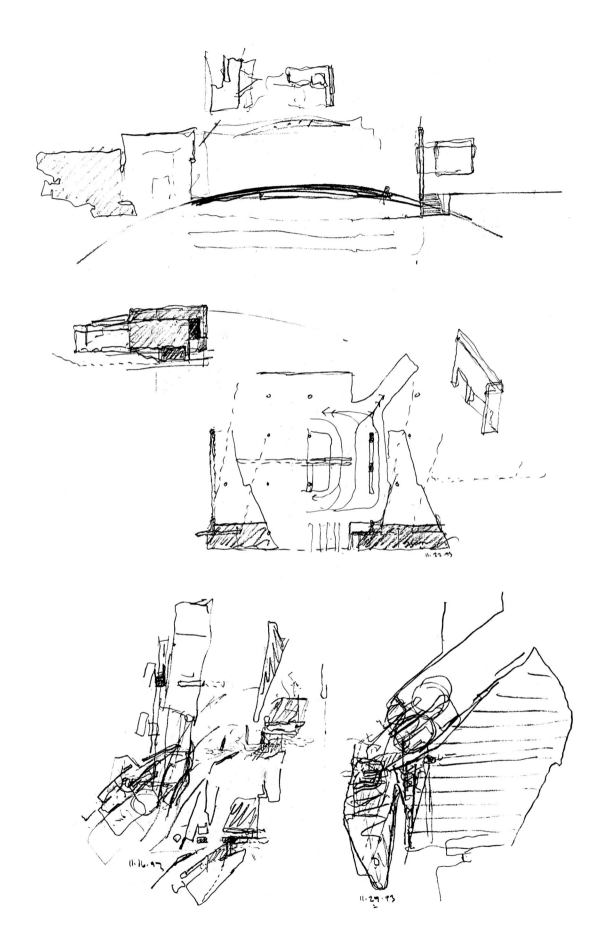

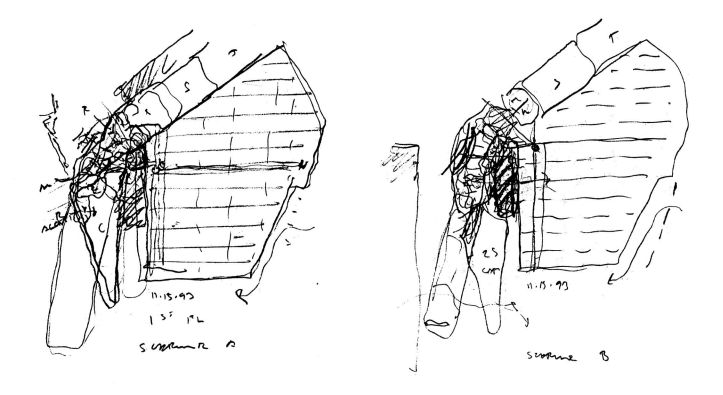

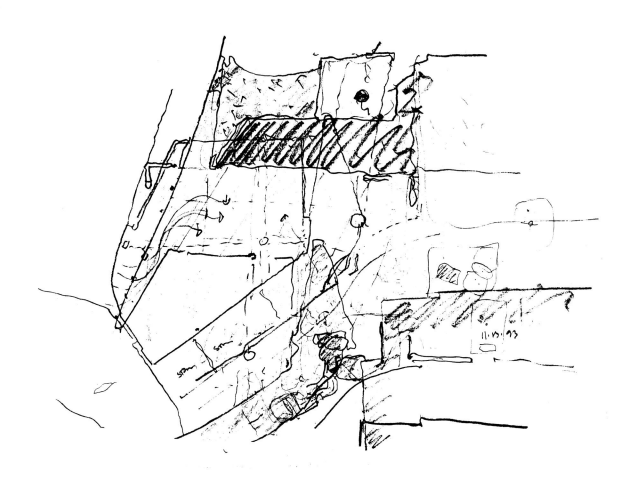

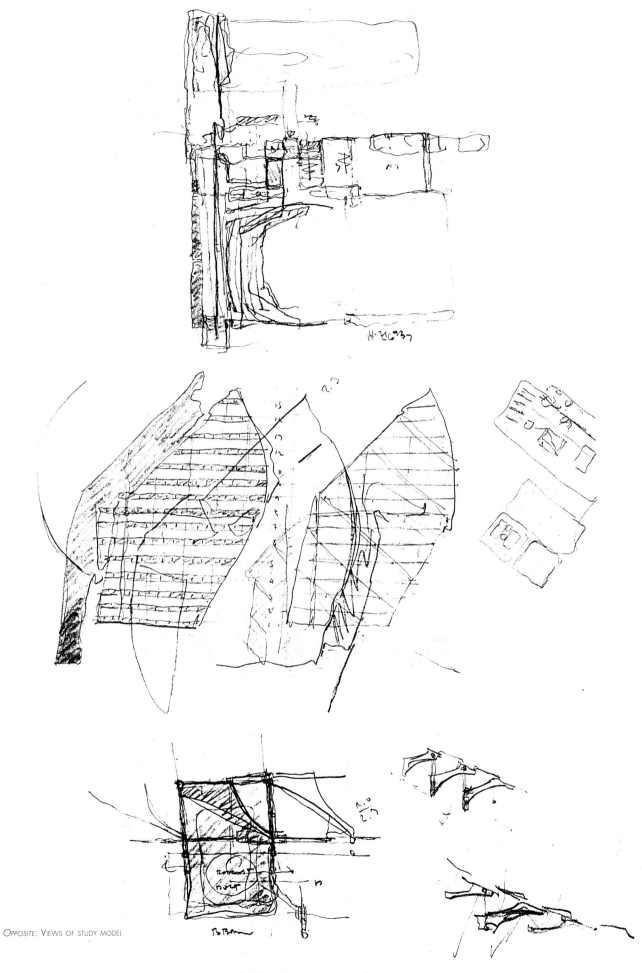

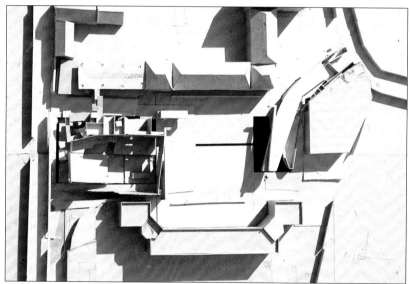

Eric Owen Moss
VLA Sun Drawing Project, VLA, New Mexico

The VLA (Very Large Array) project is a collaboration with the artist Janet Saad-Cook. The site for this project adjoins the visitor centre at the Very Large Array near Socorro, New Mexico, an international centre for astronomical research, where twenty-seven computer-controlled movable radio telescopes evaluate the skies. The building will provide space for Janet Saad-Cook's 'Sun Drawings' and will itself be an expression of the conceptual principles that are the premises of these drawings.

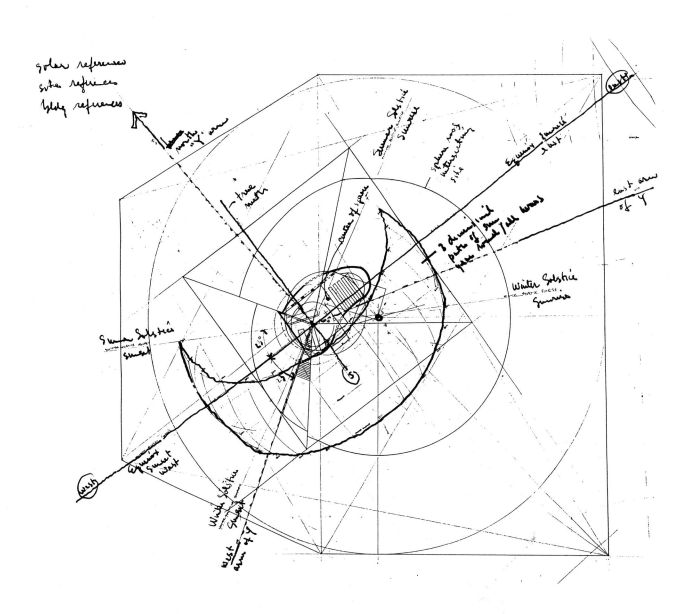

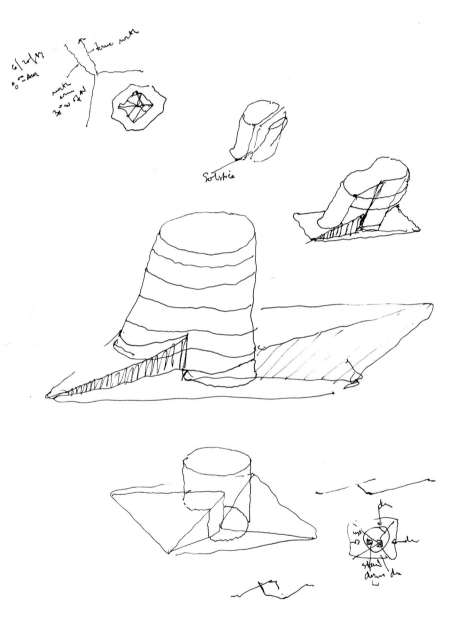

FROM L TO R: EXHIBITION HALL ON SITE;
PLAN AND SECTION OF EXHIBITION HALL,
SOLAR ORIENTED EXHIBIT WALLS COMING
THROUGH THE ROOF: SQUISH PLAN;
SECTION, PLAN AND EVOLUTION OF
EXHIBITION HALL; FROM ABOVE RIGHT:
STUDY MODEL FROM THE NORTH, SHOWING
LOWER LEVEL ENTRY RAMP; STUDY MODEL
FROM EAST END; EXHIBITION HALL FROM
SOUTHEAST, SHOWING SITE ORGANISATION

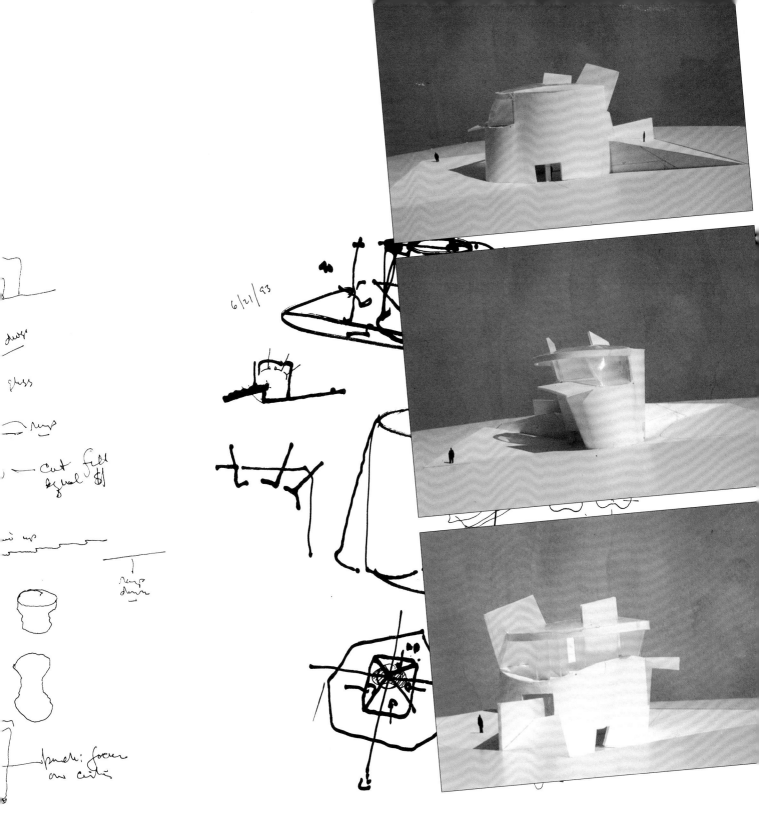

6/21/93

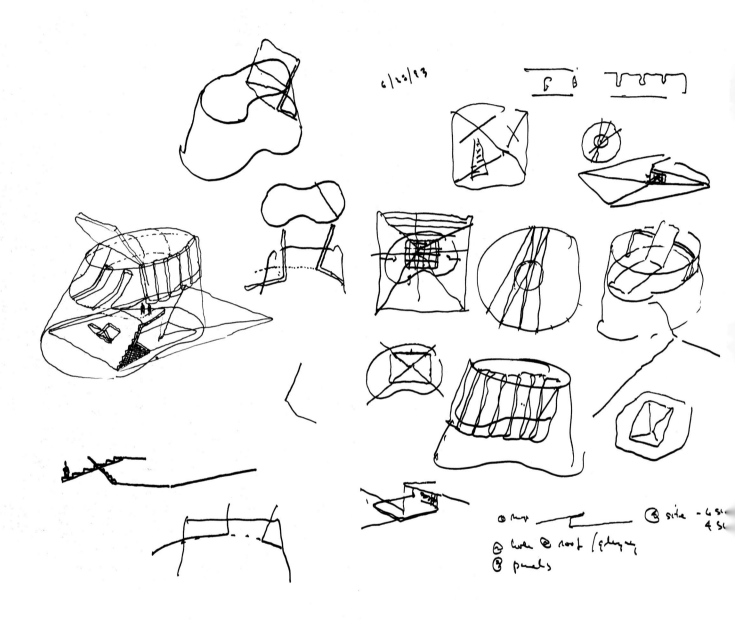

6/22/93

FROM L TO R: SKETCHES OF EXHIBITION
HALL LEVELS; THE EXHIBITION HALL'S GLASS
AND SOLID ROOFS; ROOF DETAIL OF STUDY
MODEL

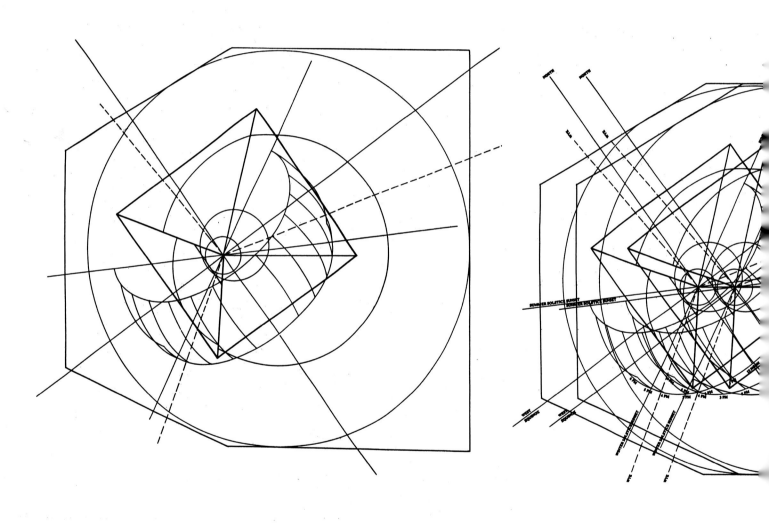

From L to R: Site study hard line; site study hard line labelled; study model from above showing raised and excavated portions, roof ring and skylights

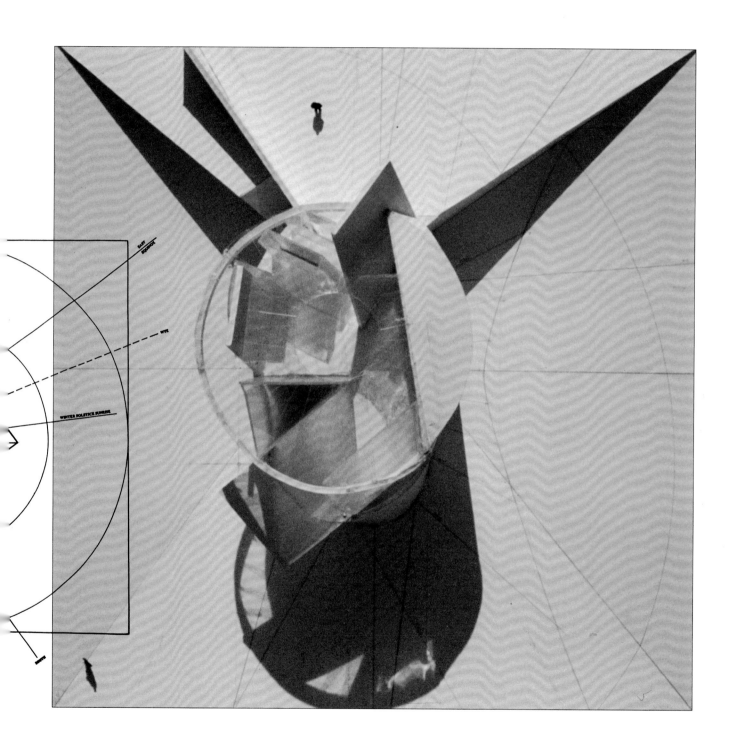

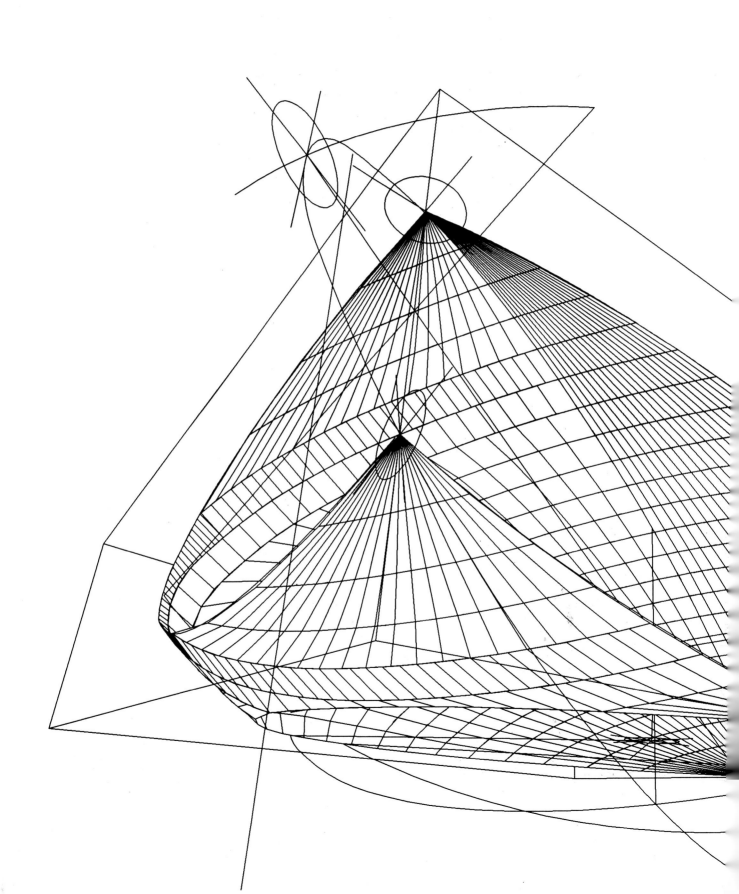

Eric Owen Moss
SMSC, Santa Monica, Los Angeles

Both the project programme and the site organisation, for the Santa Monica Science Centre (SMSC), are in the preliminary planning stages. Sketches and models are both literal and suggestive.

The focus of the project will be a two-hundred and fifty-seat planetarium theatre using a Digistar projector and software. Additional telescopes likely to be included are a coelostat solar telescope, a one-metre reflecting telescope, and perhaps a small radio telescope.

Space will be provided for conferences and exhibits. There will be a retail area, classrooms, laboratories and production space. The centre will be used by local corporations, students, scientists and the general public.

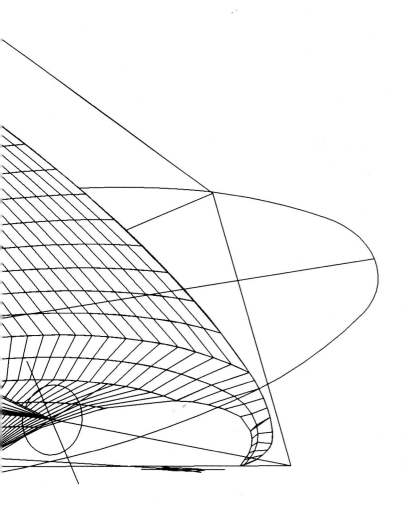

AUTOCAD 12 CONCEPTUAL DIAGRAM EVOLVED FROM ERIC OWEN MOSS' SKETCHES; *OVERLEAF, L TO R*: CONCEPTUAL STUDIES SHOWING PLANETARIUM, OUTDOOR THEATRE, PLAN, SECTION, SITE AND ORGANISATION; SITE ORGANISATIONAL ALTERNATIVES

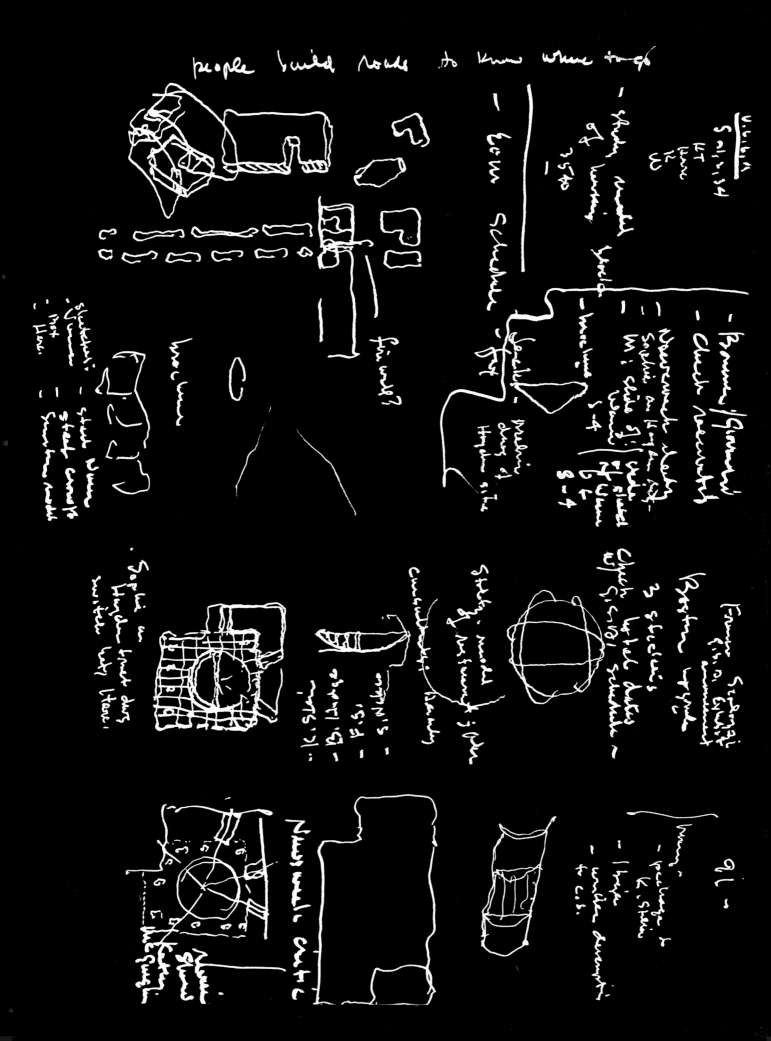

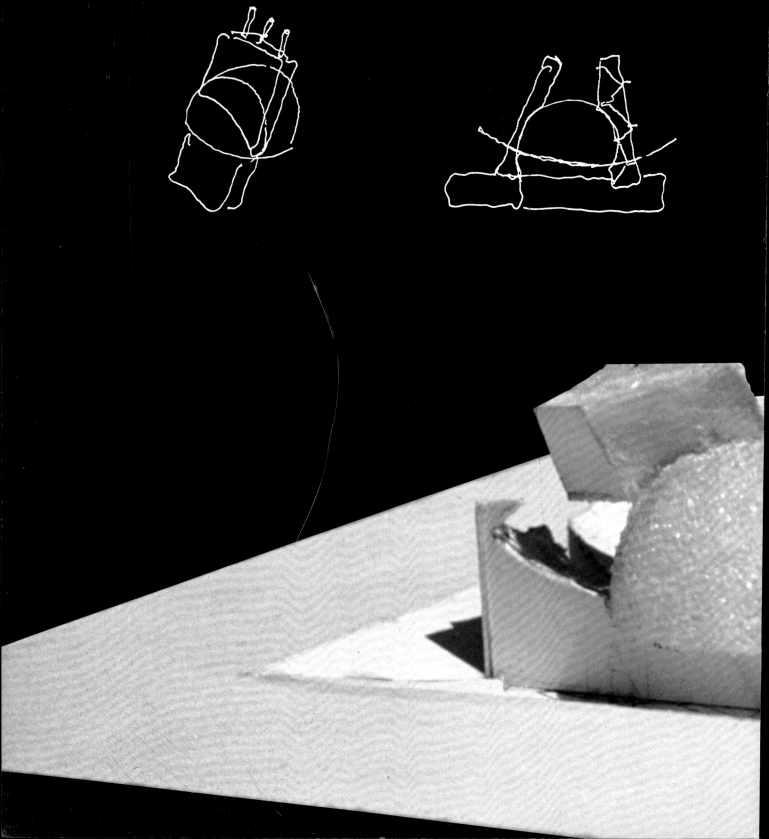

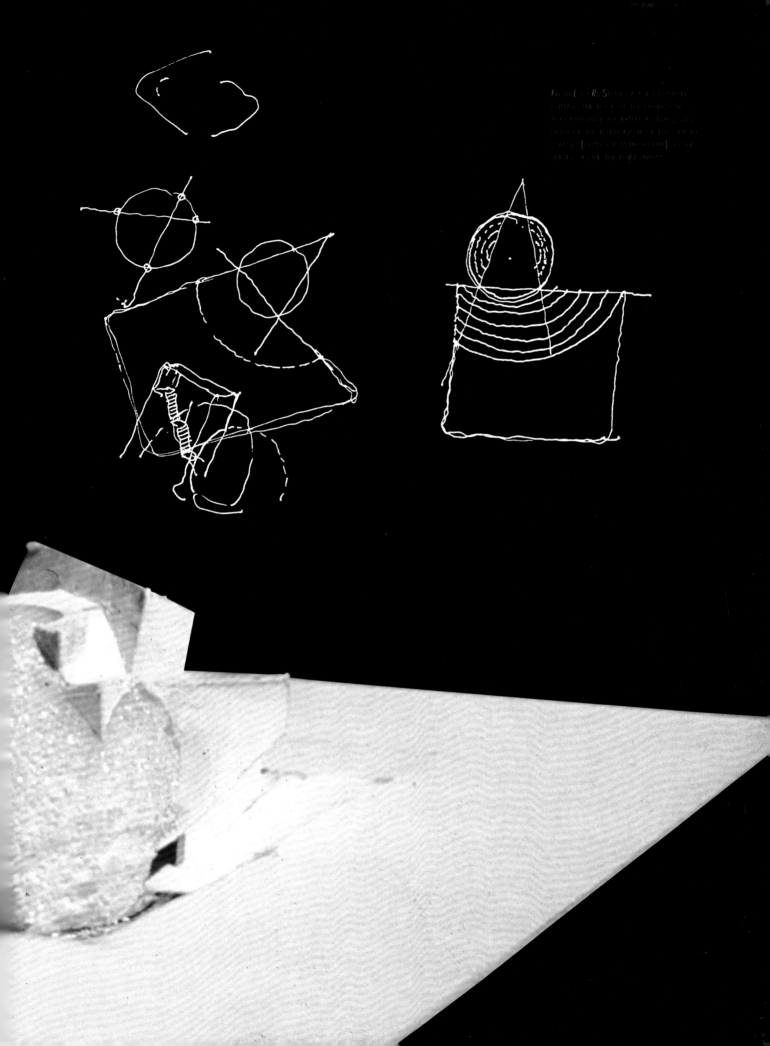

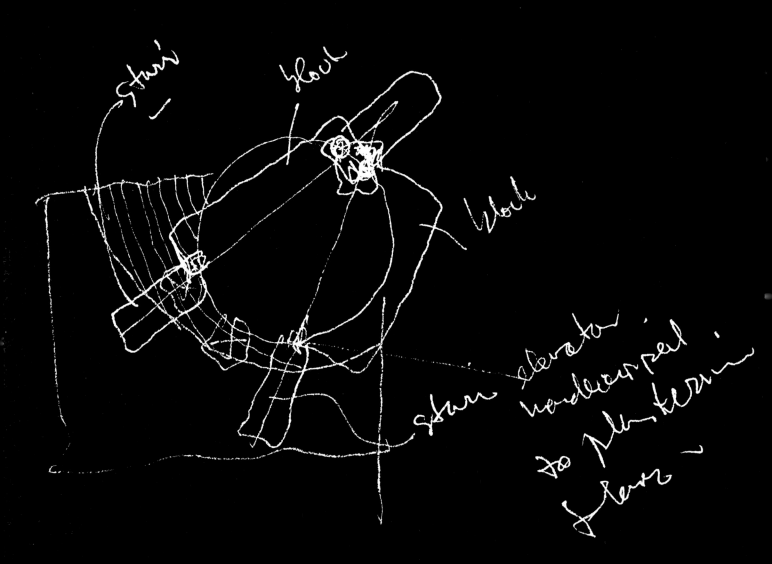

From L to R: Roof and site plan showing the organisation of telescope block, position of planetarium stairs and outdoor theatre – conceptual and geometric organisational format; intersection of the wall of the exhibition hall, planetarium, stairway to the stars and telescopes

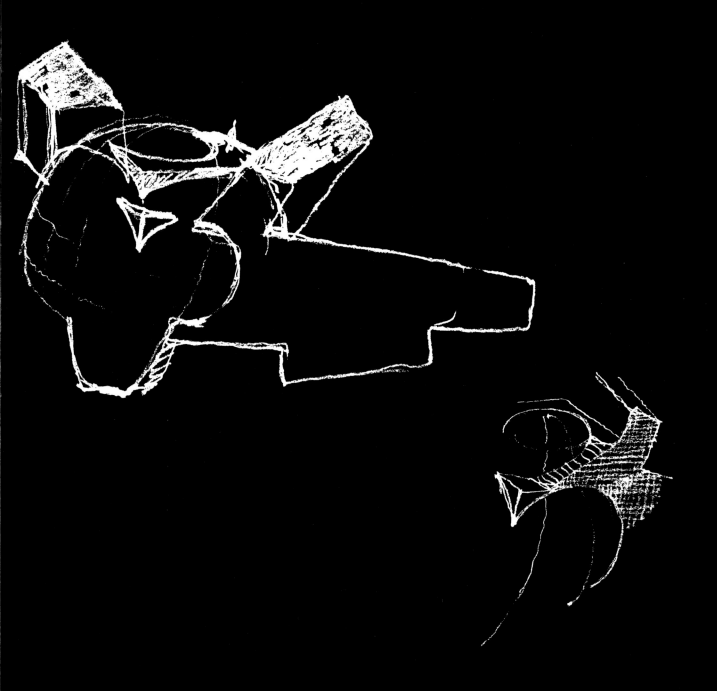

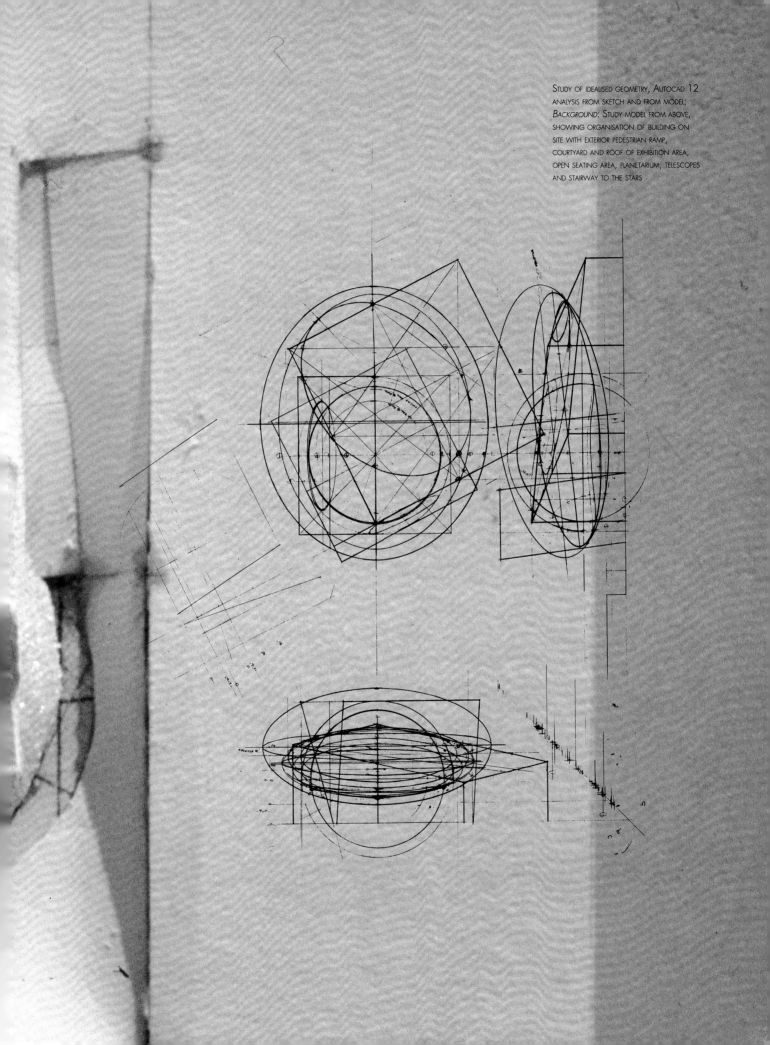

Eric Owen Moss
Nara Convention Center, Nara, Japan

The Nara Convention Center has three components – the Plaza Building (earth), the Roof Building (sky), and the Theatre Building (bridge between) – each of which has both organisational and philosophical roles in the project concept.

The Plaza Building is conceived as an open-air multipurpose plaza and garden. The space facilitates large scale exhibits of commercial or industrial products, paintings or sculpture. The plaza is carved into the earth, offering several levels of walks and gardens, and a variety of spatial experiences. Major access/egress points occur at the corners of the site. From the Sanjo-Honmachi line one enters the plaza at the south end; from the Shibatsuji-Ohmori line one enters the park at the north-west corner. Vehicles enter from the west and north. A sub-plaza structure contains parking, support space for the theatres and two skylit cafes.

The Roof Building, raised above the plaza, contains a two-level, four-way pedestrian street, a theoretical extension of the city grid.

In the quadrants, formed by the Roof Building street-grid, are a restaurant and bar, galleries, and administrative offices. The theatre structures intervene in the Roof Building, as they do in the Plaza Building. From the grid one looks at the garden plaza below and, on occasion, into the theatres.

The Theatre Buildings form a conceptual and physical bridge between the Roof and Plaza Buildings. The theatre structure originates as a parabolic curve, derived from viewing angle optimums for seats. Theatres are raised on legs above the plaza to approximately street level and are entered from either of two lobby buildings providing vertical circulation between plaza and roof functions.

Lobby buildings are accessed from the street, the plaza, or from the parking area below. Pedestrians in the plaza circulate in a landscape that combines greenery, exhibits, cafes, the stone paved plaza punctuated by concrete legs supporting the theatres and steel columns holding the Roof Building. Symbolically, the roof suggests a primitive, idealised form of both earth and sky. The building is a theoretical sphere; modified to accommodate the specifics of the city, the programme and the site.

The top of the globe is the curved roof form. The apex is cut off above the required height. The circular plan of the globe appears literally in the project only where it crosses the south-east corner of the site. The theoretical perimeter of the circle (as it traverses the city beyond the Convention Center site) defines a limit, a perimeter for extending the grid in the air, as it reconnects with the JR Nara Station, the station plaza and the surrounding redevelopment area.

OPPOSITE: CARDBOARD STUDY MODEL SHOWING BALL, RESTAURANT, TRUSSES AND FRAMING IN THEATRES FROM ABOVE; OVERLEAF: STUDY OF VARIOUS SECTION POSSIBILITIES INTERSECTING THE THREE THEATRES, THE BALL AND THE EXCAVATED LAND – ALSO SOME PLAN STUDIES OF THE INTERRELATIONSHIPS OF THE BALL AND THE IDEALISED RUBBER CITY GRID; OVERLEAF BACKGROUND: CARDBOARD STUDY MODEL FROM BELOW, ILLUSTRATING THE INTERSECTION OF THEATRES WITH THE UNDERSIDE OF THE BALL

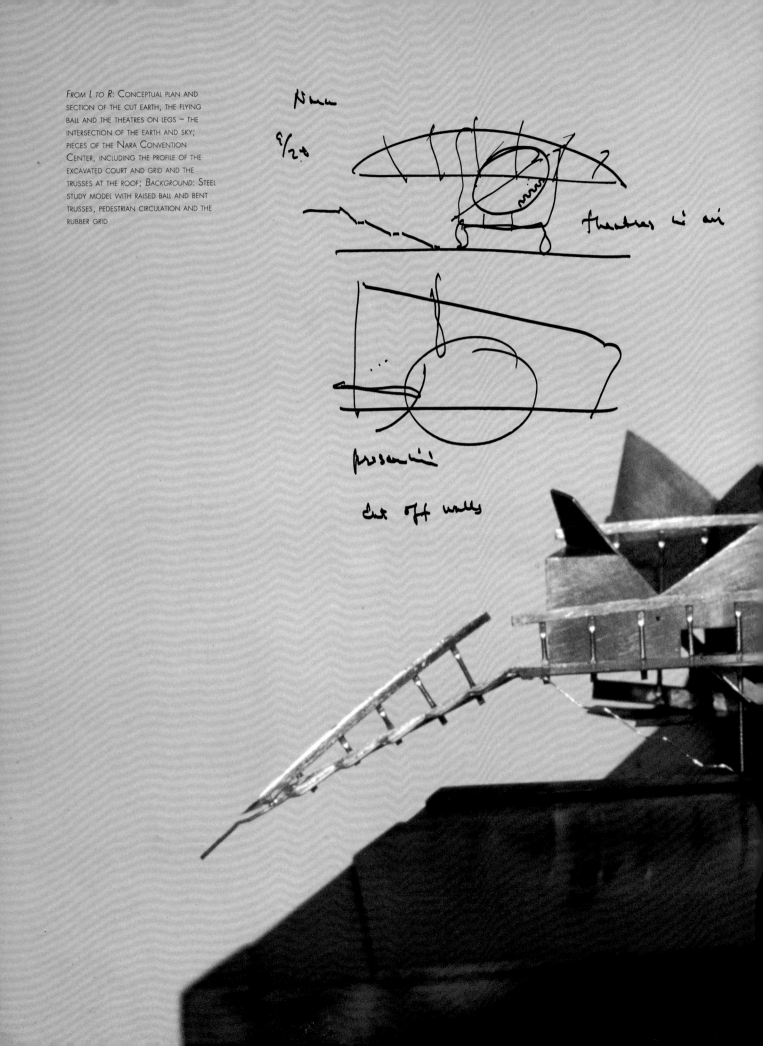

From L to R: Conceptual plan and section of the cut earth, the flying ball and the theatres on legs – the intersection of the earth and sky; pieces of the Nara Convention Center, including the profile of the excavated court and grid and the trusses at the roof; *Background*: Steel study model with raised ball and bent trusses, pedestrian circulation and the rubber grid

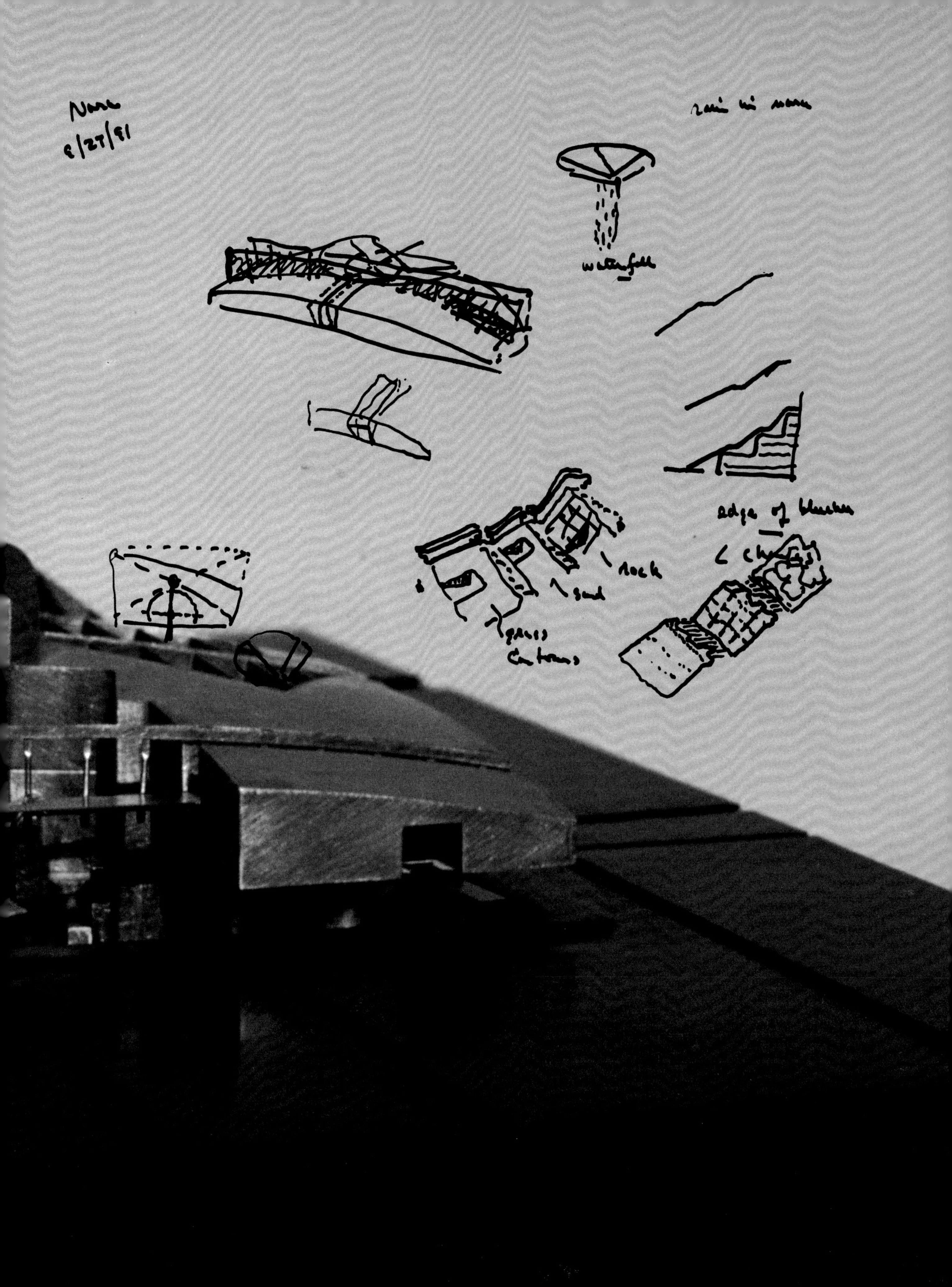
Nara
8/27/91
waterfall
edge of
rock
sand
grass
Contours

From L to R: Conceptual floor plan showing organisational relationship of the three theatres with conceptual floor plan with offices, trusses and rubber grid below; theatres in plan and in section; considering pedestrian circulation both within the theatres and outside from the street. Background: Steel study model in section, showing theatre legs and sliced ball in air, restaurant, profile in ground and the cross-the-street connection.

STEEL STUDY MODEL FROM ABOVE, SHOWING
THE INTERSECTION OF THE IDEALISED CITY GRID
WITH THE BALL, THE THEATRE FRAMING, THE
RESTAURANT AND THE PEDESTRIAN CIRCULATION
FROM ACROSS THE STREET.

Biographies of Contributors

William Alsop was born in Northampton in 1947. He was educated at the Architectural Association in London between 1968 and 1973 and is a Fellow of the Royal Society of Arts, and the Royal Institute of British Architects. During his architectural training, he was awarded the William van Allen Medal for Architecture in New York, and the Bernard Webb Scholarship in Rome.

Alsop taught sculpture at St Martin's School of Art in London (1973-81), and has been a visiting professor at colleges including the San Francisco Institute of Art in the USA, the Royal Melbourne Institute of Technology in Australia, the Bremen Akademie for Art and Music, and the University of Hanover in Germany.

The formative years Alsop spent with Cedric Price, from 1973-77, created a foundation from which he was encouraged to expand, experience and exchange ideas with other architects and artists. It is as a result of this approach that Alsop now works in close association with contemporary artists. Indeed, painting is a medium he invariably uses for initial design exploration prior to the production of architectural drawings.

William Alsop became part of an architectural European 'family' through his collaborative work with Jean Nouvel (France), Massimiliano Fuksas (Italy) and Otto Steidle (Germany). The position of his practice was firmly established in 1990 by winning the competition for the Hotel du Département in Marseilles out of a field of a hundred-and-fifty-six entries. The European aspect of William Alsop's work was strengthened by his close collaboration with Jan Störmer in Hamburg.

His work has been widely published in both the architectural and national press, covering projects such as the Leeds Corn Exchange, Tottenham Hale Station, CrossRail and the Hotel du Département. William Alsop's projects have received a number of awards, including regional and national awards from the RIBA, in 1991, for the Cardiff Visitor's Centre. In the same year the RIBA nominated this project for the RIBA Award for Architecture – Sunday Times Royal Fine Art Commission; in the following year it was short-listed for the RIBA Building of the Year award. The Leeds Corn Exchange project has received a great deal of recognition, with four awards: the Ironbridge Award, the Leeds Award for Architecture, the Design Week Award and the White Rose Award.

William Alsop has staged a number of exhibitions such as the 'Exhibition of Paintings' at the Galerie Lilli Bock in Hamburg, demonstrating his links with the world of artists. Other exhibitions include the 'Radical Architecture Exhibition', Padua, and the 'Hotel du Département, Marseille', Arc en Reve, Bordeaux.

Itsuko Hasegawa graduated from the Department of Architecture, Kanto Gakuin University, the strongest formalist school in Japan, in 1964. Since then, she has challenged the present tendency to analyse in a formalist way. Hasegawa has lectured at Waseda University and at the Tokyo Institute of Technology since 1988, and she has acted as a visiting Professor at Harvard University Graduate School of Design.

The work of Hasegawa should not be viewed simply as stimulating design; her optimism is evident in her recognition of the potential for society's transformation. Through her dialogue-based programme, an empathetic approach to architecture is made possible.

Her projects include the Shiranui Psychiatric Hospital and Stress Care Centre in Ohmuta, where Hasegawa and the client spent three years discussing the relationship between architecture and medical care to ensure a holistic architectural response. Experimental therapeutic space was achieved through the use of light reflected from the sea which also provided the comfort of the natural rhythm of the tides. Similarly, for the Shonandai Cultural Centre, Hasegawa involved the local residents, allowing for close communication between the design team and the community. Through Hasegawa's reciprocal method of planing, a new, flexible architecture can be provided that accepts a diversity of individuals.

Steven Holl is an honours graduate of the University of Washington. He studied architecture in Rome in 1970, and undertook post-graduate work at the Architectural Association in London in 1976. He has taught at Columbia University Graduate School of Architecture and Planning, New York; Syracuse University, New York; University of Washington, Seattle; Pratt Institute, New York; Parsons School of Design, New York; and the University of Pennsylvania, Philadelphia. Steven Holl Architects was established in New York City in 1976. As the firm's principal designer, Steven Holl is responsible for architectural and urban design. Under his guidance, the firm's achievements in design have been recognised internationally with numerous awards, exhibitions and special publications.

In 1989, the Museum of Modern Art presented Holl's work in a special two-man show, purchasing several drawings for its permanent collection. In 1991, Holl exhibited his work at the Walker Art Center in Minneapolis, in the series entitled 'Architecture Tomorrow' curated by Mildred Friedman. This exhibition was moved to the Henry Art Gallery in Seattle, Washington. The work of Steven Holl Architects was recently exhibited in a large travelling exhibition in Europe. Among his most recent honours are the 1993 National AIA Honor Award for Excellence in Design for 'Texas Stretto House' in Dallas, Texas, and the 1992 New York City AIA Honor Award for Excellence in Design for 'Void Space, Hinged Space' housing and shops in Fukuoka, Japan, as well as the 1992 National AIA Interiors Award for the offices of DE Shaw & Co in New York City.

Kisho Kurokawa, one of the world's most active architects, was born in Nagoya in 1934. He studied architecture at Kyoto University and gained his doctorate at Tokyo University in 1964. He established his architectural office, Kisho Kurokawa & Associates, in 1962.

In 1960 with several other people, Kisho Kurokawa formed the 'Metabolist Group' which advocated the paradigm shift from the 'Age of Machine Principle' of the twentieth century to the 'Age of Life Principle' of the twenty-first century. The key concepts, Metabolism, Metamorphosis and Symbiosis express the characteristic of the 'Ages of Life Principles'. In 1962 he became the youngest member of *Team X*, an international architecture movement started after the CIAM, which was joined by James Stirling, Christopher Alexander and Hans Hollein.

Kisho Kurokawa is also a prolific writer. As well as *Intercultural Architecture: The Philosophy of Symbiosis* (1991), which was a best-seller in Japan, his main publications include: *Urban Design* (1965); *Homo Movens* (1969); *Towards Japanese Space* (1982); *Architecture of the Street: Towards Intermediate Space* (1983); *Rediscovering Japanese Space* (1989) and *Kisho Kurokawa – From Metabolism to Symbiosis* (1992).

He has won many first prizes in major design competitions in Japan and abroad, including the New TANU Headquarters; Parliament in Tanzania; Conference City in Abu Dhabi; Al Ain University and Osaka Prefectural Government Offices. He received the Gold Medal from the Academy of Architecture in France in 1986 and the Richard Neutra Award from California State Polytechnic University in 1988. He was selected as an Honorary Fellow Member of the American Institute of Architects and the Royal Institute of British Architects.

Kurokawa's works include: National Ethnological Museum, Osaka (1977); Saitama Prefectural Museum of Modern Art, Urawa (1982); National Bunraku Theatre, Osaka (1983); Wacoal Kojimachi Building, Tokyo (1984); Nagoya City Museum of Modern Art (1987); Hiroshima City Museum of Contemporary Art (1988); Japanese-German Centre of Berlin (1988); Victoria Central, Australia (1988); Japanese-Chinese Youth Centre, Peking (1990); Melbourne Central, Melbourne, Australia (1991); Pacific Tower, Paris La Défense France (1991) and Nara City Museum of Photography, Japan (1992).

He is currently engaged in the following projects: Vincent Van Gogh Museum, Amsterdam, The Netherlands; Musée de Louvain-la-Neuve, Belgium; Osaka Prefectural Government Offices, Japan; Ehime Museum of Science, Japan; the Museum of Modern Art, Wakayama, Japan.

Thom Mayne received his Bachelor of Architecture degree in 1968 from the University of Southern California and his Masters Degree from the Harvard Graduate School of Design in 1978. He is one of the seven founding members of the Southern California Institute of Architecture (SCI-ARC), and continues to serve on its Board of Directors. He occasionally teaches thesis students, conducts special programmes and takes graduate seminars. He is currently Adjunct Professor of Architecture at UCLA.

Thom Mayne established MORPHOSIS in 1975 with the belief that design is a collective enterprise. The firm was founded with the objective of developing unique projects which focus on the multiple needs predicated by the project brief, site and client. The firm has resisted becoming specialised in any one building 'type'.

In an article about the award winning design for the Cedars Sinai Comprehensive Cancer Center, Paul Goldberger of the *New York Times* writes 'If their beginnings suggested a trendy upward mobility, it has been clear for a while that these men (and women) are among the best architects of their generation: rigorous in their thinking, humane in their outlook. Their work, which relies heavily on assertive sculptural form, often executed in metal, is both sensual and abstract, highly geometric yet never the prisoner of dogma. For MORPHOSIS, theory doesn't seem to come first: the reality of the architectural problem does.'

In the course of his professional career, Thom Mayne has received innumerable awards. Among them are the Rome Prize in Architecture in 1987, the Award in Architecture 1992 from the American Academy of Arts and Letters, and his induction into the American Academy of Fine Art in 1992. Honours as an educator include the receipt of the Eliot Noyes Chair at Harvard in 1988, and the Eero Saarinen Chair at the Yale School of Architecture in 1991.

His work has been exhibited widely, throughout California, and at the Walker Art Center, Minneapolis, the Cooper-Hewitt Museum, New York, and the Deutsche Architect Museum, Frankfurt, Germany. Thom Mayne has been the subject of many publications, from magazine articles to monographs. He continues his work at MORPHOSIS and contributes regularly to national and international architectural publications.

Eric Owen Moss was born on July 25th, 1943 in Los Angeles. He studied both mathematics and literature as an undergraduate at the University of California at Los Angeles and graduated as a Bachelor of Arts in 1965. He then studied architecture and city planning at the University of California at Berkeley, College of Environmental Design, graduating in 1968, and at Harvard University Graduate School of Design, graduating in 1972.

He began his practice in Los Angeles in 1974. During the same year he became the Professor of Design and a Member of the Board of Directors at the Southern California Institute of Architecture. He has taught, lectured and exhibited his work in the US, Japan, Europe and South America and has recently held the Eero Saarinen Chair at Yale University, and the Eliot Noyes Chair at Harvard University. He has received awards from *Progressive Architecture* among other prizes and twenty-one honour awards from the American Institute of Architecture.

Rizzoli published the first monograph on his work in 1991. Academy Editions published a second monograph in 1993. In process are books by Phaidon Press and one by Harvard University, to be published by Princeton University Press.

Moss' recent work in Los Angeles connects architecture and city planning in a series of new and reconstituted structures on contiguous sites in Culver City, between Downtown and Pacific, and Los Angeles. These projects have become a testing ground for experiments in complex geometry which are reflected in his interiors. This is most dramaticallly expressed in his S.P.A.R.CITY complex, made possible by purchase of the Southern Pacific Railroad Air Right. The singularity of his projects in this area, made possible by his close collaboration with developer Frederick Norton Smith, makes his work there one of the most extensive diagrams for a unified architecture yet realised in this region. As such it is a viable pattern for future growth. In addition, he is currently working on projects in Spain and France.